a series for
the new
Learning About Sex
6
the Christian family

Parents Guide

How to Talk Confidently with Your Child about Sex

Lenore Buth

CPH.
Concordia Publishing House

Book 6 of the Learning about Sex Series

The titles in the series:

Book 1: Why Boys and Girls Are Different
Book 2: Where Do Babies Come From?
Book 3: How You Are Changing
Book 4: Sex and the New You
Book 5: Love, Sex, and God
Book 6: How to Talk Confidently with Your Child about Sex
Book 7: Human Sexuality: A Christian Perspective

Illustrations by James Needham

This publication is available in braille and in large print for the visually impaired. Write to the Library for the Blind, 1333 S. Kirkwood Rd., St. Louis, MO 63122-7295; or call 1-800-433-3954.

Scripture quotations, unless otherwise indicated, are taken from the HOLY BIBLE, NEW INTERNATIONAL VERSION®. NIV®. Copyright © 1973, 1978, 1984 by International Bible Society. Used by permission of Zondervan Publishing House. All rights reserved.

Scripture quotations marked TEV are from the Good News Bible, the Bible in TODAY'S ENGLISH VERSION. Copyright © American Bible Society 1966, 1971, 1976. Used by permission.

Copyright © 1982, 1988, 1995, 1998 Concordia Publishing House
3558 South Jefferson Avenue, St. Louis, MO 63118-3968

Manufactured in the United States of America

1 2 3 4 5 6 7 8 9 10   07 06 05 04 03 02 01 00 99 98

Acknowledgments

We wish to thank the following for their special contributions to the Learning about Sex series:

Frederick J. Hofmeister, M.D., FACOG, Wauwatosa, Wisconsin, served as medical adviser for the series. Micheal J. Chehval, M.D., urologist and Chief of Staff at St. John's Mercy Medical Center, St. Louis, Missouri, provided an additional medical review.

Rev. Ronald W. Brusius, secretary of family life education, Board for Parish Services of the LCMS, served as chief subject matter consultant.

Kathryn Krieger and Rodney Rathmann, Day-Midweek Department, CPH, contributed special expertise in the review and editing of manuscripts.

The following provided invaluable help in their areas of expertise: Darlene Armbruster, board member, National Lutheran Parent-Teacher League; Betty Brusius, executive director, National Lutheran Parent-Teacher League; Margaret Gaulke, elementary school guidance counselor; Priscilla Henkelman, early childhood specialist; Rev. Lee Hovel, youth specialist; Robert G. Miles, Lutheran Child and Family Service of Michigan; Margaret Noettl, family life specialist; and Bonnie Schlechte, lecturer on teen sexuality.

Contents

Editor's Foreword

This book is one of a series of six designed to help parents communicate Christian values to their children in the area of sexuality. A seventh book, *Human Sexuality: A Christian Perspective*, deals with the spiritual, emotional, and physical aspects of the God-given gift of sexuality. Both the single adult and the married will profit from the practical, biblically oriented content of this last book in the series.

How to Talk Confidently with Your Child about Sex is the sixth book in the series. It is written especially for parents who want to communicate Christian values as they discuss sex with their children.

Like its predecessor, the new Learning about Sex series provides information about the social-psychological and physiological aspects of human sexuality. But more: it does so from a distinctively Christian point of view, in the context of our relationship to the God who created us and redeemed us in Jesus Christ. The series presents sex as another good gift from God that is to be used responsibly.

Each book in the series is graded—in vocabulary and in the amount of information it provides. It answers the questions that persons at each age level typically ask.

Because children vary widely in their growth rates and interest levels, parents and other concerned adults will want to preview each book in the series, directing the child to the next graded book when he or she is ready for it.

In addition to reading each book, you can use them as starting points for casual conversation and when answering other questions a child might have.

This book can also be used as a mini-unit or as part of another course of study in a Christian school setting. (Correlated video and study resources are available for both curricular and home use.) Whenever the book is used in a class setting, it is important to let the parents know beforehand, since they have the prime responsibility for the sex education of their children.

While parents will appreciate the help of the school, they will want to know what is being taught. As the Christian home and the Christian school work together, Christian values in sex education can be more effectively strengthened.

Rev. Earl H. Gaulke, Ph.D., D.D.

Now That I Have
Your Attention ...

S-E-X! Huge fluorescent orange letters on the front of the greeting card shout the word. Inside, the caption reads, "Now that I have your attention ..."

One little three-letter word. One huge concern: How can we help our children grow *with* healthy attitudes toward sex and *without* messing up their lives? How can we communicate the *Christian* view of sexuality—and do so in a convincing way? After all, we're not "experts"! We suspect that our kids already are more sexually aware than we'd like.

Let's start at the beginning, with the wonder of it all.

Fashioned by God's Own Hand!

> *So God created man in His own image, in the image of God*
> *He created him; male and female He created them ...*
> *God saw all that He had made, and it was very good*
> *(Genesis 1:27, 31).*

With tender care God fashioned the first male of the human family from the dust of the earth. Observing the man's aloneness, the LORD God took a rib from the man's chest and made a companion: the first woman.

Made in God's image. Made for each other. That's God's awesome gift of sexuality. Our loving Father means for us to delight in this blessing, but also to cherish and guard it as we would a priceless treasure.

Not What We Do, But What We Are

From that Creation day to this, our being male or female influences every aspect of our lives. Customs may change. Language may be modified. Males and females may sport identical haircuts and clothing styles. No matter. Most of us quickly distinguish between the two genders.

Controversy has raged for years over whether likenesses within each gender are inborn or acquired. Before we become parents, it sounds logical that a newborn child is rather like a lump of clay, with parents as the potters who mold and shape. Few actual parents continue to believe this charming theory, however, especially if they have more than one child. Parents of both a daughter and a son sometimes marvel. They watch their young daughter as she cuddles her baby doll or clumps around the house in Mom's high heels. They shush their little boy's continuous car-and-truck noises and note how he and his buddy seem unable to resist wrestling and scrapping. Mystified, they ask each other the perennial question of parents down through the ages: "Now where did *that* come from?"

Consider such behaviors part of the package as individuals born female or male. Indeed, many authorities seem to be rediscovering that these essential differences truly are related to the child's gender, not picked up from the culture alone. (Chalk one up for old truths proven again.) Put simply, our gender determines our outward appearance and influences our actions and choices throughout our lives.

Beware of Stereotyping!

This is not to say that every boy is like every other boy, nor every girl like all the other girls. Nevertheless, suppose we divided any group of children, boys in one cluster, girls in another. We'd find more correlations between youngsters in each gender group than between the boys and the girls. Would there be variations? Of course.

The bottom line: We are unique, with unique combinations of personality traits. Yet we also share similarities with others of our own gender.

We are male and female. Sexual beings from birth. Created to complement each other. God intended that we view our bodies and our innate sexual nature as He designed them to be when He created that first man and that first woman—as "very good"!

God's plan was, as always, perfect. Human beings, as always, have messed it up.

We Live in the Real World

Many parents admit to running scared as they contemplate guiding their offspring through their growing-up years into young adulthood. What reasonable person wouldn't be uneasy? In print, on the screen, and over the airwaves a steady parade of innuendo and blatant sex streams forth. We shudder as we consider the effect on young, undiscerning minds.

The wreckage resulting from misuse of sexuality clutters the landscape. Adults *and* children in every community are surrounded by the evidence: Marriages destroyed because of extra-marital affairs. Children bearing children. Sexually transmitted diseases (STDs) such as AIDS now accepted as a danger common to all, rather than a rarity.

We see. We hear. What once shocked us now appears "normal"—or at least commonplace. If this is true for us as adults, how much more for our children, who lack the life experience that helps foster a balanced perspective?

Questions abound. How do we steer our youngsters toward God's view of sexuality rather than society's flawed outlook? Is it even possible to raise young women and men who cherish God's precious gift *and* the marriage relationship in which He intended it to flourish?

Answers are harder to come by. Guarantees don't exist. For every human being—even our own beloved children—in the last analysis must choose and then live with the consequences.

Sex and Sexuality Are Not the Same ... Or Are They?

Sex is more than gender, more than sexual intercourse, more than "sex education." Sex is not what we *do*, but what we *are*. Actually a better term is "sexuality," for our being male or female influences every aspect of our lives, from day one. Sexuality encompasses our attitudes, our strengths and weaknesses, our whole way of looking at life. As one counselor put it, "The brain of the typical female and the brain of the typical male are wired differently. It's as simple—and as complex—as that."

To use current terminology, the logical left brain dominates the thinking process in the average male. In most females the emotion-centered right brain dominates. Neither is "better," nor is either gender "incomplete." Certainly males feel and express emotion. Certainly females employ logic and reason. It's simply that females and males *naturally* process information and arrive at decisions from a particular perspective, as parents of both daughters and sons often report.

Despite those similarities, however, beware of sweeping generalities. Within those broad parameters, individuals vary widely. Each person is God's one-and-only creation. Parents who avoid pigeonholing their children bestow a great blessing on their offspring. Marriage partners who respect and value their own and their spouse's singular gifts discover that together they're more effective than either would be alone.

Our society seems uncomfortable even acknowledging that male and female are unique. Usually media presentations either disclaim innate differences in the sexes or declare that one is "victimizing" the other. That's a setup for mutual distrust. Yes, injustice occurs, and that's wrong. Still, as Christian parents we do well to avoid echoing that dismal refrain. For every moment of every day our children are formulating their personal image, from their own opinion of themselves and from the opinions of others.

As parents, we want to provide a nurturing atmosphere in which our children can develop a strong self-image and healthy attitudes. A major factor is parental role-modeling. Do we enjoy being female or male ourselves? Do we celebrate the differences between husband and wife? between our daughters and our sons? When moms and dads delight in the uniqueness of each child God gives, children are free to blossom into secure young adults.

Changing Roles and Changeless Facts

Certainly the culture in which we live affects the choices we make. In the past, clothing styles, behaviors, and roles were clearly spelled out. Girls were told to "be nice." Misbehaving boys were excused on the premise that "boys will be boys." Today most parents bite their tongues rather than speak such clichés (even when those exact words leap to mind).

Rather we encourage both daughters and sons that they can be anything, do anything if they're willing to work hard enough. Few arenas remain unchallenged by individuals of both genders.

Yet biological differences remain. For example, despite the marvels of science, only the female can shelter the developing child within her body and physically give birth. Only the male produces sperm. Most males display greater physical strength than their female counterparts. Females generally exhibit greater endurance. As one example, females can tolerate cold temperatures for longer periods of time because they're endowed with a larger percentage of insulating body fat even when at their ideal weight.

Attitudes differ between the sexes as well. Childhood conditioning influences us markedly, whether we're male or female. Nevertheless, scientific research demonstrates specific emotional contrasts. For instance, the female is naturally more intuitive, able to balance several tasks simultaneously. Researchers report that the male typically fails to pick up subtle messages from conversation and body language, and more likely focuses on one task at a time.

Our essential male or female natures remain unaffected by whatever outward roles we assume in daily life. Variations in our talents and our emotional responses are normal. Each of us is a Designer original! (Read Psalm 139, especially verses 13–16.) Therefore, we can't lump together all males or all females, as if we were cookie-cutter images. Nor can we accurately gauge inner qualities such as strength, security, or tenderness by simple observation.

Don't Forget the Wonder!

Sexuality can't be neatly separated from the rest of life. So when we speak with our children, it's critical to remember that wide-ranging issues are part of "sex education" and of building right attitudes. S-E-X is a big topic!

We'll want to lace our discussions with a sense of wonder and joy. Wonder at the beauty of the gift God bestows on each of us. Joy that He also gives us freedom to view our bodies and our sexuality as He meant them to be when He created that first human male and female—as "very good"!

Marriage Today: Is It Better or Worse?

So the LORD God caused the man to fall into a deep sleep; and while he was sleeping, He took one of the man's ribs and closed up the place with flesh. Then the LORD God made a woman from the rib He had taken out of the man, and He brought her to the man (Genesis 2:21–22).

God created each of us a unique human being. Together the husband and wife are meant to form a complete unit. Together they're to learn from each other, balancing each other's strengths and weaknesses. God intends that the qualities inherent in one spouse find their match in the other, as with two intricately fitted halves of the same whole.

Both parents play a vital part in enabling the child to develop a healthy self-image. Day after day, children watch their parent of the same sex and determine, "Hmmm. So that's the way *I'm* supposed to act." Children also scrutinize how their opposite-sex parent treats the parent of the child's same sex. From that parental interaction, children estimate the worth of their own gender—and by association, set their own value as a person. Counselors say that adult education and discernment notwithstanding, those childish perceptions can last a lifetime.

Both Parents Play Essential Roles

Modern marriage relationships don't necessarily fit the old mold, either. Christian marriage partners want God's best: to love each other as each longs to be loved. When that's our goal, mutual cherishing, support, trust, and respect flow naturally, even though imperfectly.

Today wives *and* husbands value talk, touch, and tenderness. Once it was Mom who was in charge of hugging and counseling. Now both parents are more likely to show and to speak their love, to their sons as well as their daughters. That's good! Children flourish when they know that both Dad and Mom love them absolutely.

Marriages in which the husband takes an active role in the raising and nurturing of the children are no longer rare. Such fathers may care for infants and toddlers, handle many housekeeping chores, and do much of the cooking. Maintaining a joyful, God-pleasing marriage is not dependent on who has what role in the family.

Whatever an individual family's lifestyle, children who grow up seeing both strength and gentle nurturing in their dads are blessed. Sons grow into secure men, able to express emotion, and arrive at fatherhood knowing how to relate to their own offspring. Daughters instinctively seek out in prospective husbands the same qualities that they loved in their dads. But such fathers benefit, too. They discover the lifelong joy of closer bonds with their children.

Self-Identity Is Important

"Be an original, not a copy!" That's good advice. Still, countless adults constantly ask themselves, "Who am I?" Since each of us is "under construction," questions likely will continue. Taking time to dig out the answers enriches our lives.

First, plug in a couple of foundational truths: (1) Our value before God (and with each other) does not depend on our talent or appearance or gender (Galatians 3:28). (2) Who we are is not dependent on what we do. A male is male whether he's chopping wood or chopping carrots. A female is female whether she's toweling a baby or troweling a wall. We need to be clear on that ourselves before we can pass it on to our children.

Liking ourselves is also a necessary part of healthy self-identity. Appreciating our unique strengths is not sinful pride. For we are *God's* workmanship, *God's* redeemed children (Ephesians 2:8–10). Therefore we can be secure in our self-identity and in our relationships, whether in marriage or parenting or friendship. It's not really complicated. The more we see our own worth as a person, the more we have to give to others.

But Wait—There's More!

Day after week after month, parents model for their sons and daughters what to expect (and what to accept) from one's marriage partner. The process occurs naturally, in every family. Children take note of Mom and Dad's marital relationship in action—the talking, the smiling, the touching. Over time, young people draft a mental blueprint for their own life based on what they observe. That's why family patterns so often endure from one generation to the next.

Do we want to exert a positive influence on our children's future marriage relationship? Do we long to help ensure that our future grandchildren grow up in happy homes? Then we look to the quality of our own relationship first—not as Daddy and Mommy, but as husband and wife.

Theodore Hesburgh said, "The most important thing a father can do for his children is love their mother." The mother's love for her children's father is no less crucial. Such love-in-action bears fruit that lasts long into the future.

Without intervention, unhealthy lifestyles carry on as well. Yes, it's possible to break an old, harmful mold. But first, individuals must recognize it as destructive. Then comes determination to alter both their perspective and their acting-out. Even Christians, convinced that Christ changes hearts and transforms lives, often find such reprogramming impossible without professional counseling.

We're Supposed to Communicate All This to Our Kids? Help!

All Christian parents throughout time have sought to lay a secure foundation for their family. When it comes to presenting a godly, balanced view of sexuality, the task has never been more intimidating. Today a multitude of influences crowd into our lives, many of which can only be labeled as "evil." What can *we* possibly say that will counteract such pressure? Facing the prospect, we quake in our running shoes.

Back to basics. We build on the bedrock of faith in the Lord. *He* has not changed! We broaden our view beyond mere "sex education." Anyone can teach the usual explanation of body parts and processes. As *Christian* parents we strive to build in Christian character and moral strength. For we are caretakers, entrusted with rearing these young people.

Gently and lovingly we help our children recognize (and revel in!) their identity as both sexual beings and children of God. And we center our remarks within the context of His intention for His people: marriage and the family.

Educating about sex involves all of life, for our sexual identity permeates all that we do and colors all our attitudes. Before we fret over how to inform our children, we need to think through our own personal identity as a female or male created by God.

Next we recognize that human sexual desires and urges are not evil, although certainly humans misuse them. God created us as sexual beings. He established the marital sexual relationship (Genesis 1:28; 2:18–25). His design—that husband and wife come together as one flesh—is meant to cause us to celebrate and to thank God.

If struggle mars either marriage partner's physical or emotional response, it's time to seek help from a qualified counselor. (It's wise to check with a pastor or family doctor for names, rather than choosing from an ad. And there's no cause for embarrassment! Rather we should be proud and thankful that we value our marriage relationship highly enough to work on it.) Too often parents assume that their own relationship is private. Mom and Dad kid themselves that as long as they watch what they say, their children will never even notice their difficulty, and can grow up unaffected.

Not true! Children see through the most carefully maintained masks. Pretense and subterfuge, even when well-intentioned, smack of hypocrisy to young people. Less emotional damage results when parents admit, "Yes, we're having some problems. You don't need to know the specifics. We're working on them, because we want our marriage to last forever!"

Children and teens can handle such truth, even when it's troubling. They already know that imperfect human beings make mistakes and say hurtful things. Witnessing first-hand that love and marriage can weather such storms provides a useful lesson they can file away for the future.

What If I Can't Get the Words Out?

Talking about sex with our own offspring makes many of us uneasy. Adding to our discomfort is wondering whether our kids mentally substitute "Dad" and "Mom" when we speak of "male" and "female." What if they want to know whether *we* did that or whether that's what *we* do when we're alone and the bedroom door is locked? Even if they don't voice such questions out loud, we realize that our darlings are no dummies. So we squirm a bit.

Part of our uneasiness may stem from the concept of The Official Parent-to-Child Talk about Sex. Sounds like a solemn occasion, guaranteed to strike us with stage fright! Sometimes parents put off casual questions from their children by saying, "We'll talk about that later." That, of course, increases the pressure for anxious parents.

So let's get rid of the scholarly lecture. Besides, it's more effective to use teachable moments, like the natural questions that arise during a young child's bath time. Shorter explanations, one at a time, are easier for the child to assimilate—and for the parent to give.

In any case, one confidence-builder is to be armed with the facts. It's helpful to study the diagrams and terminology in this book, as well as the other books in this series. Our goal as parental educators is to come across as fairly knowledgeable about how the human body works. But we lose no credibility when we say, "I don't know the answer, but I'll find out." (Unless, of course, we never mention it again.)

As for stumbling over words, if we haven't talked much about sex before we'll probably feel (and sound) shaky at first. Don't worry! We'll have lots of time to get better at it. Discussing sexuality with our growing children is like anything else: Practice pays dividends.

We're on Stage 24 Hours a Day

It's impossible to overstate this principle: Mom and Dad's marriage relationship, both emotional and sexual, remains the major factor in the attitudes their offspring develop.

For parents teach about life and love and sex all the time. Children *absorb* more than they'll ever hear said in any parent-child talk. That's as true for the very young child as for the high-schooler. For our kids watch us all day, every day. They listen to our adult conversations and our off-hand remarks. Over time these youngsters formulate their values and plan what they'll be like … someday.

That's a truth that mandates an honest assessment of ourselves— our everyday attitudes and behavior. For example, if Dad or Mom put each other down, they are *teaching* their child how to relate to one's marriage partner. Parents teach when they laugh at sexual jokes or racy TV plots or say, "Way to go!" upon hearing accounts of celebrity sexual exploits. The single parent involved in a sexual relationship teaches that wedding rings are unnecessary.

It's as if young people are working on a complicated jigsaw puzzle. They add one piece here, another there. They're searching for what it means to be a male, a female, a marriage partner, a parent. As parents, we are to our children like the illustration on the cover of the box the puzzle came in. Our kids constantly check the image they're piecing together against how we relate—as husband and wife, as parent to child.

There's no escaping the truth. Parental explanations of sexuality, no matter how wise and skillfully stated, carry little impact unless reinforced by the child's firsthand observation of the parent. It's that basic—and that difficult.

So what do we do if our self-examination reveals that personal changes are in order? We call on our God, who promises to make all things new. Then we talk through with our youngsters the mistakes we've made, the lessons learned, and our new resolve. (There's no need to get too specific. General terms will do nicely. You may need to answer some questions with, "I'm sorry. That's personal.")

Do we long to provide a powerful example of how Christians deal with their failings and make changes? What better way than to apologize to our child when we've been impatient with her—or selfish or vindictive or less than loving in other ways? And then also ask for her and for God's forgiveness. Similarly, we can lead our child to admit his failings and to look to God's forgiveness in Christ for healing and strength. "Confess your sins to each other and pray for each other so that you may be healed" (James 5:16).

But What If I'm Alone?

Both the widowed and the divorced single parent feel the strain of having no partner with whom to discuss problems and pool wisdom.

Wise single parents constantly check their own motives and actions to be sure that they're not unconsciously turning their child into a substitute spouse. (This is not to suggest a sexual relationship. Rather the trap for lonely adults is that they begin to depend on their son or daughter on an emotional level that's inappropriate.) No child can—or should be expected to—meet the parent's needs.

Divorced single parents face a special challenge. Perhaps feeling discarded, the temptation is strong to enlist the child as an ally. Accusations and bitter talk against the ex often become the weapons of choice. "Letting it all out" may provide momentary relief of tension for the parent, but it's not wise for the child to hear such tirades. That son or daughter, lacking maturity and experience, may assign blame not only to the absent parent, but to that entire gender. Or the hurting child may shut down emotionally, determined never to be hurt as the parent was hurt. Either way, the resulting damage to the child's view of sexuality and marriage may be lifelong.

Meeting the Challenge

How to balance the equation when only one parent is present in the home? Ask trusted friends and relatives of the opposite sex to invest themselves in the life of your child. Allow yourself to be vulnerable with fellow church members. Seek their input and their suggestions. Be bold enough to ask other parents to include your child in their family activities, and offer to do the same for them.

Single parents can and do raise healthy, emotionally well-balanced children, but it demands determination and extra effort to do so. The task also requires that you speak well of marriage, even if your own marriage did not endure. For you want your child to grow up believing that a solid marriage is both desirable *and* possible.

What about My Social Life?

Single parents may or may not choose to date. Many counselors advise against allowing children to become emotionally attached to the person one is seeing, unless there are wedding plans. For if that relationship breaks up, the child once again feels the pain of being abandoned. Naturally the hurt goes even deeper if the person has lived for a time in the same house and become, in effect, a substitute parent.

Some single parents bring their lovers home to sleep over or ask them to move in. The fallout is the same, with or without a planned marriage. In each instance, the parent sends a powerful message to the child: "Sexual intercourse without marriage has my personal seal of approval, no matter what words I may *say* to you." Scratch the parent as a credible role model for sexual morality.

How could it be otherwise? Living proof of that unspoken message is present under the same roof, every morning and every evening. Parental explanations and justifications are a waste of time. Admonitions to postpone sexual activity until maturity won't be heard. Here, as always, the number one principle of parenting applies: *No words speak as loudly as personal example.*

Take Heart!

All parents, no matter what our situation may be, require a lot of help. Thankfully, as Christian parents we have a loving, forgiving Helper who walks this unknown path with us and picks us up when we stumble.

Yes, our task as parents *is* daunting! What do we do? First, last, and always, we pray. Second, we avoid the trap of assuming that either we or our children are helpless victims. God is our strength and our help, the same for us as for those first parents in that smaller society. Third, we remember that outside influences are just that: *outside*. Of far greater impact is how Mom and Dad live and speak and act, day after day.

Married or single, we can't duck the issue. Our example to our own children is of prime importance. They watch us for proof that we mean what we say by living it out in our own lives.

Someone has said, "What you are speaks so loud that I can't hear what you say." No more insightful statement on parenthood could be made.

Necessary Equipment

It's a given that we'll make mistakes. So as we travel the road of parenting, one essential for the journey is a sense of humor. Another is honesty—with God, with ourselves, and with our marriage partner. Being humble enough (and honest enough) to admit our failings, even to our children, is a plus. Most of all, we rely day by day on the forgiveness we have in Christ.

Christian couples, pledged to making their relationships blossom, can be a powerful witness in the world. They can exemplify what God intends marriage to be: the union of two people in a lifelong commitment to be faithful and to serve each other, growing as individuals and as a couple, and living in love.

As in all of life, we look to God for guidance and enabling. After all, He created us, male and female, and He admired His handiwork. Since He also redeemed us and is recreating us in His Son, can we do less?

Children = Changes

Sons are a heritage from the LORD, children a reward from Him (Psalm 127:3).

It's a familiar scenario. Childless couples who field "baby" questions from well-meaning friends and relatives often explain with great sincerity, "We're waiting until the time is right to start a family."

Invariably that remark evokes chuckles from seasoned parents who reply, "There *is* no right time! Trust me, you'll *never* be ready for parenthood!"

Ain't it the truth! Who among us could foresee that such a tiny bundle of humanity could turn our world upside down?

Subtle changes begin when the woman misses that first menstrual period. Immediately both partners find their perspective on life enlarges. The husband ponders what it will mean to be a father. The wife ticks off the months to wait and thinks about the bodily changes that lie ahead. Together they try out names and speculate about the future. In a word, they become child-centered.

Reality comes through loud and clear soon after the baby is born. Before too many days elapse, the exhausted new mom and dad begin to suspect the truth: Life will never be as it was before.

For example, it's a shock to discover that the "helpless" newborn infant reigns supreme. The baby screams for service, and everyone jumps to answer the summons. No matter how dearly they love their newborn, before long the bleary-eyed parents look at each other and wonder, "What kind of path have we set out on?"

Think of this phenomenon as a form of consciousness-raising. From the day the child arrives, parents embark on a constant learning adventure. Each phase of the child's life is new to both child and parents. Each child in any given family is unique, so a parent's prior experience may count for little. The learning goes on for life!

The Number One Task

The most important task that faces the new father and mother is *not* the obvious physical child care and support. The major job, starting with Day 1, is to provide their child with constant, accepting love. As Christians we believe that kind of love has only one source: God.

> Dear friends, let us love one another, for love comes from
> God. ... We love because He first loved us (1 John 4:7, 19).

No less vital is to have the same attitude toward each other. When parents feel loved themselves, they have an abundance of love to give their offspring. In such an atmosphere, children are more likely grow up well-adjusted, with good self-images and the foundation they need for their adult lives.

The child's sense of being accepted or rejected, his or her self-image and value system for the rest of life, is greatly influenced during the first five years of life. Stay-at-home parents may see those years as a period of confinement and hard work, with never a moment to call their own. (And in many ways that's true.) Yet all the time, life values are being laid down.

When both parents work away from home, it's of prime importance that there is as little turnover as possible in the person(s) providing child care, for a child needs stability. It's also vital that the person(s) who care for children have attitudes and values to which parents themselves subscribe. A child often spends more waking hours with a baby-sitter than with his parents, so that person's lifestyle and views inevitably carry great weight with the child. Is that reassuring? Or does it make us uneasy?

Reading this may fill many of us with remorse and guilt. If so, be assured: All parents make mistakes. All parents have times when they feel antagonism toward their child. All parents at times communicate attitudes they later regret. And few totally agree with their baby-sitter's attitudes, even when the child's own grandparents fill that role. So what's a parent to do?

"There's only one thing parents can do!" says Great-Grandma. "Same as we did and our folks before us. That's just ask the good Lord for wisdom and count on Him to take everything in our children's lives—even our mistakes—and turn them to good. He did it in Bible times. He still can!"

Our Children Copy Us

Each of us is a model for our children, day after day, year after year, whether we wish to be or not.

What do we want our children to become? What do we want them to remember? No matter what we answer, the truth is that our children's strengths and weaknesses, the values they will have, and their sexual attitudes are determined more by what they see in us than by any other single factor. The timeworn expressions we've all heard are true:

- More is caught than taught.
- What you are speaks so loudly that I can't hear what you say.
- Our children are only entrusted to our care. Although part of us, they don't belong to us in the sense of possessions. Nor are they an extension of us. They are individuals in their own right.

Children Are Sexual Beings, Too

It may be surprising to realize that our children are sexual beings from birth. For instance, a parent changing a male infant's diaper may accidentally stimulate the child and be shocked to realize the child is having an erection. Similarly, researchers tell us that baby girls have vaginal lubrication regularly. In fact, a little girl being bounced on her parent's knee may feel pleasant sensations and begin to make natural pelvic thrust movements.

This is *not* to say we should be afraid to touch our children or bounce them on our knees! It's merely to point out that all of us are born as sexual beings. Yet somehow the thought of a child's sexual nature is vaguely disturbing to many adults. We've all known, of course, that children ask questions about where babies come from, etc., but we've assumed this is simple curiosity. We may answer in great detail yet feel uncomfortable talking of such things with our youngsters. Children are naturally curious, true, but their sexual nature plays a part in such questioning, too. It bears repeating: We are created by God to be sexual beings, from the very first day of our lives.

Those Important First Two Years

During the first two years of life, children get their foundation—the establishment of their own gender and that of others, plus role behavior; a sense of body and self-image, along with motor coordination; a feeling of closeness with (or estrangement from) other humans, especially parents; a realization they are welcomed into the family and accepted by those around. We build a sound, healthy base for the child by ample touching and closeness. "Sex education" takes place every day, as we interact with our child.

Words and facial expression carry weight, too, even with very young children. For instance, some parents teach their toddler the name of every body part except the child's genitals. What message does that send? When young children explore their genitals, either absentmindedly or intentionally, parents overreact. Yet would we say "Don't touch that!" or slap their hands if they touched an ear? Besides, kids are curious, and these interesting areas usually are covered up.

During this stage of life as with all others, the most important influence is how the parents relate to each other, how they view their own sexuality. Far from being oblivious, the young child is constantly watching, evaluating, assimilating.

Laying a Strong Foundation in the Preschool Years

Jesus said, "Let the little children come to Me, and do not hinder them, for the kingdom of heaven belongs to such as these" (Matthew 19:14).

From ages 3 to 6, the child's picture of what it means to be male or female is strengthened. This forms a basic sense of appropriate behavior and begins to be part of the child's approach to life.

"Kevin and I used to think it was cute when our little girl and boy played house," said Belinda, "but when we really began to listen, it wasn't funny! 'Daddy' spent all his time in front of the TV, telling the 'children' to be quiet. 'Mommy' did nothing but complain about how tough her life was—how no one cared how hard she worked.

"One day we asked Aaron what a man does. He said, 'Well, he's gone a lot. When he comes home, everybody has to be quiet so he can rest. Daddies don't have to do anything at home.' Then we asked Alissa what a woman does, and she said, 'A woman does all the work, and nobody ever helps her unless she hollers. She never has time to play games or go the park. And she looks mad all the time.'

"Once we realized what our children were learning from watching us, we decided to make some changes," continued Belinda. "Neither Kevin nor I liked the picture they were giving us. But it was simply a reflection of what our kids saw and heard."

As Belinda and Kevin found out, children learn their roles—what it means to be a male or female—by watching us, and then they pattern (model) themselves after us. This is especially true during this age period, when children have fewer outside distractions. In fact, the parents' example is the central factor in the child's *self-identity development* from the very beginning and is imbedded for life.

Although the child identifies mostly with the parent of the same sex, the other parent has an important influence, too. For instance, a girl gets her idea of what a male should be largely from her father—or from another adult male who plays a major role in her life (an uncle, a grandfather, etc.). She also receives reinforcement of her own feminine nature. The same kind of thing occurs with boys and their mothers.

But children learn more than just role behavior from their parents. They either learn a loving God has a part in their daily life—or they don't. They also adopt emotional qualities such as a caring attitude or one that implies, "Don't bother me"; concern for others or insensitivity; love or coldness; kindness or belligerence; generosity or selfishness; patience or impatience.

Individual differences do count, but so does environment. For instance, a family's gloomy temperament may not be so much a hereditary trait as a behavior pattern acquired during the parents' childhood and passed on to the next generation.

Outside Influences

If our child attends a day-care center, a nursery school, or a preschool, it's vital that we evaluate especially the school's teachers and helpers to determine their values and goals. We'll want to observe how staff members relate to the children—and each other. We'll look—and listen—to discover whether personnel and other children display the behavior and healthy attitudes we desire in our own child.

From time to time the news media carry reports of abuse, both physical and sexual, by day-care providers. Surely the majority of child-care providers are trustworthy! Nevertheless, no parent can afford to take for granted that *all* owners and staffers are trustworthy.

As responsible parents, we'll want to ask about background checks of those employed. We'll obtain personal references from the owner(s). We'll ask for names and phone numbers of parents whose children currently spend time at the facility—and for a couple of parents who've taken their children out after a time. Then we will take time to call these individuals and to ask those blunt questions that may make us uncomfortable.

In addition, we'll want to spend time just watching and listening, and also interviewing personnel. If the rules prohibit drop-in visits by parents at any time, we'll lose no time in walking away.

Although this may seem time-consuming, it's the only way to relative peace of mind. After all, what's more precious than our children?

Besides, one of the young child's basic needs is constancy in child care. The youngster's stability is reinforced by long-term, secure relationships. That makes it advisable to do as much advance evaluation as possible, in order to avoid relocating the child frequently.

Preschoolers Are Curious about Sex

When the three- to six-year-old asks questions about sex, answer calmly, in the same manner and tone of voice as with any other subject. Give basic information, using correct terminology. Too often parents feel uneasy using terms such as *uterus, vagina,* and *penis.* So they may say something like, "The baby is growing in Mommy's tummy" or speak vaguely of "a seed from the father being planted" in the mother.

As a result, the child may have troubling mental pictures of the baby growing in Mommy's tummy, alongside a cheeseburger and french fries. Or memories of digging and helping to plant seeds in the garden may cause a child to wonder how that has any connection with Mommy and Daddy. Therefore, it's important to emphasize that the uterus, which is near the stomach, and the vagina are special places in a woman's body, made by God for a unique purpose.

No need to get clinical, though. Remember the mother in the old joke? When her three-year-old asked, "Where did I come from?" she immediately launched into a detailed explanation of conception and birth. When she paused at last and asked if he had any questions, the little boy said, "Yeah. But what was the name of that town where we lived before?"

In other words, answer the questions that are asked. Children will absorb only what they are ready to understand, so no great harm will be done if we over-explain. Sharing a book with your child can be helpful, too. Book 1 of the Learning about Sex series is written just for this age group. In *Why Boys and Girls Are Different,* author Carol Greene delightfully captures a child's sense of wonder about sexuality, God's creation, and the warmth of family life.

———————— **Questions from Parents** ————————

Child Sleeping with Parents

Our three-year-old has developed a habit of coming into our bedroom in the middle of the night and crawling into our bed. Is this harmful?

Taking a fearful child into your bed on occasion will not cause problems. If this becomes a habit, however, it could be one that is hard to break. After all, it's important that parents have some time alone together. (If not in your own bed, then where will you find it?)

Still, there are no hard-and-fast rules. Some parents never allow their child into their bed, while others have a "family bed." Even with newborns, some mothers want their infant in bed with them, some prefer the child's crib in the parents' bedroom, and some can't sleep themselves unless the child is in a separate room. Parents are free to discover what works best in their own families.

There are a couple of cautions. The young child who must be with parents *all* the time easily can become emotionally over-attached to the parent(s). It's also possible that a child may experience some feelings of sexual arousal, which could be confusing, even though the parent has done nothing to cause it. Don't look for that, but be aware. Then again, a child may deliberately try to come between parents, literally and figuratively. The child may appear delighted to plop down between Mommy and Daddy, but such action may involve competitive feelings with the parent of the same sex. (Such feelings are common at this age.)

Child Interrupting Parents' Intercourse

Our child walked into our bedroom while we were having intercourse. How should we have handled it?

Young children—even infants—can be confused by seeing or hearing their parents engaging in sexual intercourse. The child may interpret the movements, sounds, and facial expressions as violence similar to wrestling, fighting, or in some way hurting each other.

If your child walks into your bedroom unannounced, in the midst of intercourse, stop what you're doing and reassure your child. Offer a brief explanation—perhaps something like this:

"Daddy and I love each other very much—you know that. And sometimes when we're together we want to hold each other very, very close—to touch each other all over and almost be a part of each other's body. That's the way God made married people. It's one way we show how much we love each other.

"We love you, too, but we want to be alone now, so please go back to bed. And from now on please remember to knock on our door and wait for us to answer before you come into our room, because this is our private territory."

Establish a family policy early. Impress upon family members that courteous people always knock when doors are closed—and that includes parents as well as children. A lock on your bedroom door is an obvious solution, of course. In any case, emphasize that your room is off-limits unless the door is open.

Nudity in the Home

Is it harmful for children to see their parents and/or siblings nude?

There is no right or wrong for the young child. If the parents are comfortable with their own standards, the children will be, too. If children are accustomed from birth to seeing their parents nude, there will likely be no effect at all. Of course, children may have questions about their parents' bodies; for instance, a boy may want to know why his father's penis is larger than his own or a girl may wonder why she doesn't have breasts like her mommy. Parents should answer such questions casually, reassuring the children they will also develop as maturity approaches.

Most siblings are quite unaware of each other's nudity in the early years. They usually accept each other's anatomical differences with little note once they've had their initial questions answered. Children vary greatly in their personal sense of modesty. One child may be disturbed when a sibling (or parent) sees them unclothed, while another cares not at all. Respect the right to privacy of the uncomfortable child, and insist that siblings do, too.

As children get older, they should be brought to realize that modesty requires some restrictions on nudity, even in the seclusion of the home. For example, as your preschoolers get older, should they happen to catch you undressed, simply ask the child to leave the room until you're dressed. Even in the most relaxed family, common courtesy demands that every family member respect a closed door and knock before entering.

The other day I found my three-year-old and my five-year-old examining each other's sexual organs. How should I deal with it if it happens again?

Remember that young children are inquisitive about everything— and that includes their sexuality. Such games and general exploration are common in these years. The children may undress and may touch each other as well as themselves. Girls may play with girls, or boys with boys, but this is not assumed to indicate homosexual tendencies.

Even though curiosity is the primary force, children's normal response may include pleasure, which we parents find unsettling.

Stay calm and low-key. Say something like, "God gave us beautiful bodies, didn't He? I know that you're curious about each other's bodies 'private parts.' To keep something private means that we don't show it around, or let other people touch us there. I don't want you to ask to see their private parts, either. God made your body very special and wonderful—and very *private*.

"So if you want to know about how our bodies work, Honey, or have questions, I hope you'll come add ask me or Daddy (Mommy). Now why don't you two put your clothes back on, while I get out that game you like to play?"

Find an activity that keeps them busy—whatever will distract them. You may want to supervise a bit more closely for a while. Unless you feel such sexual play is becoming obsessive or addictive, there's no cause for concern.

Six to Nine:
Carpe Diem

Train a child in the way he should go, and when he is old he will not turn from it (Proverbs 22:6).

Seize the moment! This period is prime time for imparting values and establishing good habits. Infancy and the toddler years, with their consuming dependency, are history. Children often are excited about new learning skills. Usually kids this age love doing things with their parents and still consider parental wisdom reliable. The roller-coaster ride of adolescence lies comfortably off in the horizon.

What better opportunity for us to communicate our own faith, our values, and why we hold them? For example, how does our faith relate to our family life and our way of living? As always, our words carry little weight unless backed up by example. So we *go with* our children to Sunday school and worship services. We read the Bible often, on our own and with them, so that they perceive the value of drawing on God's Word. If they've heard us praying for them (and see us praying alone) they already realize that talking to God is important. For children this age, our task as parents is to help them lay a foundation of faith that will last a lifetime.

And time grows short! Once children start attending school, the circle of people influencing them widens considerably. Their teacher may become the supreme authority on everything. Children also develop close friendships with peers, who exert a powerful influence. Their perception of how to behave as male or female may change as they have more contact with families having differing lifestyles.

Because children of this age group are not yet involved in dating, not yet experiencing personal sexual attraction, they'll accept our explanations and values more readily than in the future. For that reason it's a prime time to develop healthy, relaxed attitudes toward sex.

Parents should answer questions about sex calmly and frankly, but also look for opportunities to offer such information when the child has not asked. Open communication is not the total answer, however. Most attitudes that children adopt come more as a result of copying someone they admire, especially their parents.

"The child guidance class I took was a big help to me," says Gwen. "It made me realize that no matter how crazy the world seems sometimes, no matter how many factors affect our children, Mark and I are the most important, most lasting influence of all. Our kids get most of their ideas of how to be a man or woman—a husband or wife—from watching us.

"My friend Dina, who's a widow, was quite disturbed. After all, she's raising her children alone," continues Gwen. "But the teacher made us see that other people who are part of the wider family circle—like Dina's dad and her brother and the next-door neighbor—can also be good male role models. Understanding that helped ease her mind. Sure made us realize, though, how important it is to be careful about the people spending time with our children. They may be personal friends, but if we wouldn't want our kids to copy them, we'd better arrange to see those people at other times."

A Time of Curiosity

Children this age are curious—about everything. So you may find them "playing doctor" one day, giving you a natural opportunity to offer sex information. If you discover such play, be casual about it and avoid imparting—or implying—guilt or shame.

You might want to say something like, "Well, Joshua, I suppose you and Beth wanted to see if little girls and little boys are alike. Now you know that boys and girls are different. God made all boys the same and all girls the same."

This would be a good time to offer a positive substitute activity. You might want to say something like, "How would each of you like a glass of milk? Want to come out in the kitchen and help me get things ready for lunch?"

Talking about Sex

In the above situation, you may not want to talk in more detail unless both children are your own. If so, this would be an excellent time to go into more detail, correctly naming parts of the body. (Otherwise speak to your own child when you're alone.)

You may wish to say something like this: "God gives all boys special body parts that make them boys. One part is called a penis. When you urinate, Joshua, you use your penis. The water, which we call urine, comes out through a tube called the urethra, which is inside your penis. The tube is something like a soda straw. Girls have a urethra tube, too, but it's up inside their bodies, and the urine comes out through a little opening.

"Boys also have two testicles. They're shaped a bit like eggs. The testicles are enclosed in a sac of skin called the scrotum, and they're just behind the penis. Your body is getting ready now for when you grow up, Joshua, when you may want to be a daddy. The seed for making babies, which is called sperm, will come from the testicles and go out the penis.

"You probably noticed that Beth is different. That's because God gives girls special body parts, too, but inside their bodies where you can't see them. Beth has a special place called a vagina and another special place called a uterus, just like every other girl.

"One of the things a girl can do when she grows up is to be a mommy. Babies grow inside their mother's uterus, safe and warm, until they're big enough and strong enough to come out through the vagina and live on their own. That's the way you got here, you know. You grew in Mommy's uterus, and when you were all ready, you were born. And everybody loved you so much and was so happy to see you!"

Such an explanation will help to reinforce the child's self-identity as male or female—and also the feeling of being a loved, wanted part of the family. If it seems unnecessarily detailed, remember that it's wise to use correct terminology, remembering again that at any age children filter out what's beyond their understanding. On the other hand, if your child asks for more information, such as how sexual intercourse happens, feel free to enlarge upon this explanation.

Don't forget that children even in the lower grades commonly are exposed to sexual information as a part of their school curriculum. Schools vary greatly as to what topics will be covered and in what depth. As responsible parents, we have the right to check with our children's teachers and ask to see the text(s) to be used. It's important to allow time to read them with care.

What's being taught may surprise or even shock us. But if we're forewarned and informed, at least we can discuss the material with our children, based on our Christian perspective.

This can also be a good time to share a children's book with your son or daughter. The books in this series are written from a Christian perspective. Book 2, *Where Do Babies Come From?* by Ruth Hummel, is written for children in grades 1 and 2. For children in grades 3 through 5, Book 3, *How You Are Changing*, by Jane Graver, would be appropriate. Read these books with your child. Be sensitive and ready to answer questions your child may be too timid to ask. Make it a special time of sharing and closeness. Once you're sure the child understands the content, you may wish to let your youngster keep the book for private rereading.

Self-stimulation

It's not unusual to find children from six to nine years touching their genitals frequently, perhaps for prolonged periods of time. Again, the child is behaving in a completely normal, natural manner. But at this older age we may associate such masturbation with deliberate sexual action, and thus we may feel more uncomfortable with this behavior than earlier. How do we deal with it?

As always, a calm, casual approach is best. For if we say something like, "Nice boys (or girls) don't touch themselves there," the child may decide that particular area of the body must have something nasty about it. This can negatively affect sexual attitudes.

Perhaps we may notice self-stimulation occurring repeatedly. It may be an absentminded activity, such as when the child is watching television or is simply bored. In fact, many counselors believe that a child who lacks enough association with others and/or spends long periods of time alone is more likely to indulge in self-stimulation as a habit. (If you feel masturbation is becoming obsessive—that the child is addicted to this activity—seek counseling.) Most of the time simply adding more structure to the child's life will help. Assuring socialization with others—both inside and outside the family—will provide positive alternatives.

Setting Limits

The six- to nine-year-old is becoming more responsible. As we allow privileges and set restrictions, consistency is essential so children know the limits. We parents needn't be uneasy about saying no, if that's our well-considered decision. Rather we should be cheerful but firm, explain our reasoning, and resolve to help our children gradually learn to deal with increasing freedom, as they demonstrate their ability to handle it. After all, that's one of the tasks of parenthood.

Facing the Challenge of Parenthood

Many parents looking back over the years think they would like another chance—that they would be wiser the second time around. The challenge of parenthood is enormous, and we know we'll make countless mistakes over the years. Yet we can accept it with complete confidence. How?

- By daily asking God's guidance and trusting His will for our lives.
- By entrusting our children's development to God's care rather than simply to our own knowledge and skill.
- By telling our children over and over that we love them.
- By demonstrating love through frequent gestures of affection. ("Have you hugged your kid today?")
- By liberally praising our children's efforts. (As one mother puts it, "One pat on the back is worth a dozen pats on the rear!")
- By accepting our children as unique creations of God and trusting Him to round off the rough edges.

———— Questions Parents Ask ————

When Does Puberty Begin?

My eight-year-old daughter insists that her best girlfriend has to wear a bra because she "bounces" when she runs. Isn't nine too young for signs of puberty?

According to government health statistics, the onset of puberty continues to drop. One recent large-scale study indicates that nearly half of black girls and 15 percent of white girls begin to develop sexually by age eight. Somewhere around age 12 still is considered average for the onset of menstruation. But it's no longer rare for girls as young as age nine to begin their menstrual periods.

So now's the time for that parent-daughter talk you envisioned as safely tucked away on your agenda for the future. At this age you'll need to give only the basics, so your daughter doesn't pick up misinformation. From time to time you'll want to revisit the topic, so that your daughter will be prepared emotionally. You may wish to say something like this:

"Honey, you're growing up so fast! Have you noticed that your body seems to be changing? When you notice that your breasts are growing, and that hair is starting to grow between your legs, your body is sending signals of what's coming. This is exciting, because it means that you're on your way to becoming a woman.

"I can't say exactly when, but probably you'll be about 12 years old, maybe a bit older, maybe a bit younger, when one day you find that there's a bit of blood on your panties—or perhaps on the toilet paper. That means that your body is beginning the process of menstruation. Menstruation is not like an injury—it doesn't hurt like when you bleed from a cut. It's a happy sign that your body is getting ready for you to be an adult woman!

"If you're here at home, come and tell me or Dad (Mom). Or if you're at school, go talk to your teacher or to the school nurse. Usually it's three to four days before the bleeding stops, and you'll need to wear a sanitary pad during that time. I've bought you your own box, so you'll be ready.

"Once menstruation begins, you'll have a menstrual period about once every four weeks for years and years. Every month when you menstruate, remember that this is part of God's gift to you. You see, God designed you to be a female. Little by little, your body is getting ready for you to be an adult. The menstrual blood passed every month is put in the uterus to prepare it to nourish a baby. Someday you may find the man you love and want to be married to for the rest of your life. God's plan is that adult females are the ones who can become pregnant and give birth, then nurse their babies with milk from their own breasts. So you'll need a grown-up body if you and your husband want to have children. And you'll love them so much, just as I love you! Just think, when you have babies, I'll be their Grandma (Grandpa)!"

You needn't go into more detail at this age unless your daughter asks questions.

Explaining Intercourse to a Grade-Schooler

My grade-schooler knows about reproduction, but I guess I should explain about sexual intercourse. How detailed should I get?

If children in this age group grew up far from the influence of TV and the movies, most would have only a passing interest in sex. However, the typical kid in the typical home today is more sexually aware than youngsters of previous generations. Children are big consumers of television programs and movies. Sexual comments and innuendos permeate most television shows and movies, even some identified as "children's programming."

Furthermore, youngsters often watch over and over videos or favorite cable television programming aimed at children and youth. So we have the repetition factor added to the involvement of *two* senses when children view whatever is before them on the screen. To use a popular term, today's children have their consciousness raised.

In the rare household without television, there's still the sexual information routinely presented in the classroom. Sex education classes and AIDS-prevention classes are standard, even in the lower grades. Children may know about body parts and bodily functions. However, don't suppose that they understand the sexual *relationship*.

The good news is that most kids this age haven't begun to personalize sexual topics, so they're not yet self-conscious. Count on getting some exceedingly frank questions from your offspring. Welcome their questions and comments! You'll never have a better time to plant healthy, Christian attitudes about sex.

It's assumed that you've already given your child basic information, including correct names for body parts. Still, the child may have only a hazy memory of what you said or may merely need to hear it repeated. Listen to the question and answer honestly. Don't proceed with a long discussion for every simple question.

A young child may observe pets mating (which, by the way, is good background) and ask, "Do men and women ever do anything like that? Is that how people get a baby?"

Answer casually, something like this: "Those animals are mating. At certain times animals have the urge to mate, and they may mate with many different animals during that period. God made people different, though. He gave us love for each other, not just feelings called instincts. When a husband and wife want to have a baby or perhaps when they want to show that they love each other very much, they have what's called sexual intercourse. When they're all alone and feeling really close, the husband puts his penis into his wife's vagina. It's a very special thing, just between the husband and the wife."

A child this age may just say oh and go out to play. Or the next remark may be something like, "Do they like it? Does it hurt?" You may even get questions such as, "Did you and Daddy do that to get me? Do you ever do it now?"

Again, answer matter-of-factly, something like: "When two grown people love each other, it doesn't hurt and they like it very much. Yes, that *is* how you began—with a tiny part from Mommy called an ovum or egg and a tiny part from Daddy called a sperm. When these two met, they formed one cell inside Mommy's body and you started to grow inside Mommy's uterus—a special place where you could be safe and warm until you were big enough to live on your own.

"When God made men and women, He gave them this way to show they love each other. So the answer to your question is yes. Daddy and I have intercourse, because we care about each other very much."

Letting children know that parents have sexual feelings—and that they treat them as a natural part of living—assures youngsters that sexual expression is a normal ingredient in life. They'll mentally file this knowledge. It will help them cope with their own sexual feelings in coming years.

Your child may well ask random questions—one today and another six months from now. Take such questions in stride, answer them honestly, and enjoy this stage of your child's life. Because children don't yet personalize sexual information, this is a great opportunity to lay a strong, solid foundation for the healthy attitudes of a lifetime.

Try to appreciate the openness of this age. In a short while you'll be wishing you knew what was going on in your teenager's mind!

Exhibitionism

There's a man in our neighborhood who's a known flasher. How can I prepare my daughter in case he should confront her?

The exhibitionist gets sexual gratification from exhibiting his genitals to unsuspecting observers. The typical case is a man who delights in showing himself to young girls. Obviously this is not normal behavior, but at least your child is not in physical danger. Most exhibitionists remain a safe distance away from their victims, and exposing themselves is their sole activity.

Such people are often called "flashers," and they hope to shock their viewers. Therefore, any female confronted by a flasher is well-advised to act as though she's ignoring the entire performance.

Impress on your daughter that such a male is sick and needs psychological help. Tell her that she'll probably be surprised and perhaps a bit frightened, but reassure her that *probably* she's in no danger. After all, you may tell her, it's no big deal to see body parts. If she can see the situation as rather silly, it will help. And if she can feel pity for the exhibitionist who must get his kicks from such behavior, she'll probably be fine.

Although flashers usually pose no threat or harm, she needs to walk away from such a person and come tell you or another responsible adult.

Usually a child will accept such a parental explanation and that will be the end of it. Should your child seem wary and nervous as time goes on, seek help from a counselor.

As for the flasher, you'll want to report his behavior to the police as soon as you become aware, so that he can be helped.

What about Pedophiles?

Are pedophiles the same as flashers?

No. Flashers display their genitals, and seldom do more. Pedophiles, however, prey on children, first establishing a friendship, then a sexual relationship. Most such men experience no guilt, convinced that in such sexual involvement, the adult is doing the child a favor. These individuals may or may not be homosexuals.

Pedophiles obviously are seriously disturbed. They seldom appear to be anything but normal, caring guys who love being around children. That's precisely what makes them so dangerous. Pedophiles typically seek out children who seem insecure or emotionally needy. For example, a youngster may be worried because parents are fighting, or may be desperately hungry for attention, usually from an adult male. Such a child, of course, responds gratefully to extra attention and apparent understanding.

Pedophiles often look for an opportunity to be with children, sometimes through their work, sometimes in volunteer organizations. As parents, we can't go through life suspecting every man who works with children. On the other hand, we can't assume that every man who works with youngsters is operating out of sound motives and is a safe companion for them.

So as responsible parents we'll want to check out *any* adult who works with our children. Trustworthy advisors in community organizations and programs will rejoice that we take an interest and want to safeguard our child. We'll observe interaction between adults and children, ask questions, and *think*!

Counselors stress that emotionally secure children are less at risk. One protective measure is to ensure that our children know they are loved—no ifs, ands, or buts. Another is to help our youngsters develop their natural talents or to learn a skill or sport, so that they feel good about themselves. It's wise to talk with our sons and daughters about what constitutes appropriate behavior between adults and children.

If we're raising our child alone, we'll search out ways in which loving, trustworthy adults can interact with our child. The single parent who has concentrated on becoming self-sufficient may find it difficult to admit need. But here's a place where the end justifies letting down our guard and asking a friend, relative, or fellow church member for help.

One more point: In every situation our kids need to know that they can come to us with *anything*, assured that we'll respond lovingly and will check out their concerns. So before we dismiss their comments with those easy words, "Oh, I'm sure _____ didn't mean anything by that," we need to ask more questions and solicit additional information.

Sexual Abuse and Incest

Sexual abuse and incest are in the news all the time. How can I talk to my children about these topics without frightening them?

First, let's be clear and broaden the term to include *any* unwanted sexual contact or stimulation, not just intercourse.

Most sexual child abuse is carried out by a member of the child's own family (incest)—a stepfather or father, an uncle, a sibling, a grandfather, or a cousin. In blended families the risk of sexual abuse is almost double. Stepbrothers as well as stepfathers are the most frequent abusers.

Contrary to popular opinion, the child abuser may be a "pillar of the community" type. In fact, Scout leaders, teachers, and even Sunday school teachers and pastors have been convicted of child molestation. Typically it's an older male with a young female. Most victims are molested in their own home or that of someone they know and trust.

Such activity can occur very early, long before the girl's body begins to develop, and may continue over a period of years. Most girls don't tell anyone about it—because they love the person involved, because they don't want to make him and/or their mother angry, because they've been threatened, etc. But they know instinctively that something is wrong, so they begin to feel ashamed and responsible in some vague, nameless fashion. And they almost always turn that guilt in upon themselves. This can cause emotional and spiritual problems.

(Young boys are also subject to abuse, mostly from men or older boys who may or may not be related.)

It's important to give a child some guidelines, but to avoid instilling fear or suspicion: "Your body belongs to Jesus and to you. People may shake your hand or hug you or kiss you or pat you on the back, and that's fine because that's how we show you we love you! Or sometimes you may go to the doctor and he (she) has to check you over from head to foot, and that's okay because that's his (her) job.

"But other people don't have a right to touch you when you don't want them to—or to touch you around your vagina (penis). God planned that we wait until marriage to touch or be touched by another person in these private parts of our bodies. So nobody else should touch you where your swimsuit covers your body. And *nobody* should try to make you touch them there either, even if an adult says it's okay.

"If anyone ever does try to touch your vagina (penis) or asks you to touch theirs, say NO! and get away from that person. It's okay to scream or to run away if you have to, even if that's the person who's in charge. Come and tell me, or some other grown-up you trust. I promise not to get angry with you. I want you to know that you can tell me anything. Anytime something makes you sad or upset, I want to know it."

Then be ready to listen! Police and social workers say that children often say they tried to tell a parent, but she or he was "too busy." Let your home be a place where your child feels opening up to you is safe. Take your child's thoughts and feelings seriously. Suppose your child says, "I don't like Mr. Smith! He's weird!" You could immediately respond, "You shouldn't talk like that!" Or you could gently ask, "What makes you think so?" Choose the latter style, and you're much more likely to get a glimpse into your child's mind and heart.

It's essential, too, that children know they're loved by their parents, and that includes giving them lots of hugs and kisses. Yet as their children grow taller and begin to fill out, parents may be uncomfortable and withdraw their open affection. Even the adolescent who's 12-going-on-25 may perceive this as rejection. Inevitably, the young person struggling to grow up then becomes a bit lonelier, a bit more vulnerable, perhaps depressed. Child molesters seek out children who fit this description, ready to shower them with attention and gifts. The molester then becomes the adult who "really cares" about the susceptible child.

Become a detective if you notice any of the following signals in your formerly secure, well-balanced child: She/He exhibits continuing fearful behavior; becomes excessively moody or dependent; acts out sexual movements or seems somehow focused on sexual behavior and innuendoes; displays physical indicators such as itching, discharge, bruises, etc. in the genital area.

Parents walk a fine line. We can't suspect every possible child abuser, but we need to be watchful. Planting fear in our children is unwise. Rather, the goal is to give them a healthy caution and sense of control over their own bodies. That includes the right to refuse to kiss someone. (If the child repeatedly objects to the same person, respect that emotion and find out what is behind the child's action.)

Adolescence: On the Way

Even a child is known by his actions, by whether his conduct is pure and right (Proverbs 20:11).

Some youngsters change overnight. Yesterday they were children. Today they appear as teenagers. "It seems like yesterday that Jana was a baby," says Becky wistfully. "Now she's 12 and losing her baby fat, developing a womanly shape. Her personality seems to be changing, too. Sometimes she's so grown-up and responsible I say to myself, 'All those years of hard work are paying off.' I can really get a glimpse of the lovely young woman I hope she'll become. I'm proud of her—and of myself, I guess, because I think I've been a pretty fair parent.

"But then she'll turn around and do something so childish I can't believe it!"

Most parents of youngsters in the 10 to 14 age group can identify with Becky's feelings. These are years of rapid growth and change. Even the previously most stable, well-balanced youngsters become unpredictable. Parents are seldom prepared for this emotionally, even when warned. It's a time when parents need faith—not only in God but also in their children.

Underneath the turmoil, however, we can understand what's happening. Our children, though often puzzling and/or frustrating to us, have not really become strangers, haven't actually changed so much. What we see now are the temporary changes that are part of adolescence. The foundation we've been laying so carefully over the years is still there, whether plainly visible or not. And it can be continually reinforced by our prayers.

The Time of Awakening

From ages 10 to 14, the child's own sense of sexuality is stirring.

This is the age when many girls have intense friendships with other girls and boys with boys. But girls have begun to look at boys with interest, and boys are thinking someday soon they just might want to get close to someone soft and feminine—someone besides their mothers. As one 12-year-old boy put it, "If I ever stop hating girls, she'll be the first one on the list!"

This can be an unsettling time for young people. Their level of hormone production is changing rapidly, and emotions fluctuate greatly. All sorts of surprising things are happening to their bodies, too, like the growth of hair under their arms and in the pubic area. To the dismay of adolescents (and parents) no amount of anti-acne cream stops zits. It's common for young people this age to become self-conscious, and some develop an excruciating modesty.

Girls note, usually with satisfaction, that their breasts are rounding. Some are upset to notice only one breast swelling (almost always a temporary condition) and may wonder whether they'll ever be "normal." The shape of the girl's hips changes, and she has her first menstrual period. And if she seems obsessed with her breasts and hips—continually wondering why one or the other can't be larger or smaller—relax! She's just a typical adolescent girl. But she needs your assurance that she's attractive as she is, that her body is just right for her.

Boys' bodies are changing, too, although less noticeably. A boy may be dismayed to see his breasts swelling and/or the nipples hardening. (He needs reassurance that this is normal and won't last long, even if he doesn't ask about it.) He's embarrassed to discover his penis gets stiff at times, and he may begin to have nocturnal emissions (wet dreams), probably around age 13. His voice may change.

Youngsters of both sexes are often depressed to find acne blemishing their formerly smooth complexions. This, of course, is usually due to the fluctuating hormonal levels and will settle down once they're stabilized. To make matters worse, young people have all sorts of thoughts that simultaneously frighten, intrigue, and please them.

What's a parent to do? Prepare them well in advance for these normal, natural body processes. Knowing what's happening to them—and why—will lessen many anxieties. But take it one step further. For example, boys should be told about menstruation, and girls should also hear the facts about boys. For example, researchers have identified live sperm in the semen of boys as young as 10. That means, of course, that such a boy could father a child. Both boys and girls should be made aware of this possibility, even though it may be remote.

Girls need reassurance, too, that increased white vaginal discharge is normal. They should also be prepared *early* for menstruation. Today it's not uncommon for nine- and ten-year-olds to begin menstruating, and the average age of onset is in the 11-year-old range. The young girl whose first knowledge of menstruation comes when she discovers blood on her panties can be thoroughly frightened and bewildered.

Talking about Sex

Adolescence is unpredictable! As parents, sometimes we're not sure whether our offspring are "young" or "old" for their ages. Variations in maturity mean that any timetable must be interpreted in light of the individual child. One youngster is ready for in-depth discussions of sexual topics quite early. Another of the same age is uninterested and immature. Both are normal!

Yet as parents, we agonize over when to say what. Since precise guidelines are impossible, it's up to us to adapt the level of discussion to match the level of our own child's maturity. Discussion-starters are meant to be just that. Topics covered can be pared down or enlarged to fit, revisited from time to time throughout the child's teen years. In every case, we as parents make the judgment call.

Unfortunately, parent-child communication about sexual matters often ceases during these years, just when it's needed most. "I get all tongue-tied. I know what I should say, but I can't get the words out," said one mother. "I keep thinking that perhaps I'll just give the children ideas," said a father. "Maybe I'm wrong, but I wonder whether they should hear all that stuff now. You know what they say— 'Ignorance is bliss.' "

But ignorance is *not* bliss. When parents fail to communicate information and their own values, their children simply go elsewhere. They ask their friends, they avidly watch television and movies, and they may read morally base books. So we parents have to weigh our own awkwardness in talking with our children against the misinformation and distorted values they'll almost surely gather elsewhere.

Good books can be helpful here. *Sex and the New You*, Book 4 in the Learning about Sex series, talks frankly about bodily changes and immediate concerns of this age group.

Such a book can provide an opening for conversation, once the child has read it. Or it may serve as a good follow-up, to reinforce knowledge gained during parent-child communication. But no book is an adequate substitute for heart-to-heart talks with a loving parent.

During such conversations, it's well to be frank about our own feelings. "It's silly, I know, but I was petrified when I finally got up the courage to talk to my oldest daughter," confessed Christine. "I wasn't covering my discomfort very well, so finally I just admitted it. I explained that I was self-conscious because I'd never been able to talk to Grandma and Grandpa when I was young—and I really wanted to talk with her. Somehow that broke down the barriers on both sides, and from then on it was much easier for both of us."

When talking with our children, we'll want to answer questions about sex with absolute honesty. If a particular question stumps you, say, "I don't know the answer, but let's find out together." Don't mention only body parts, but talk also about your feelings about your own sexuality. Speak of your personal values, how love is expressed in family relationships—between husband and wife, by establishing your home, and by loving and caring for your children. Try to convey that sexuality is a gift from God and not to be abused. If you feel uncomfortable, admit it and forge ahead.

Classes Are Not Enough

Some parents—and certainly many educators and other authorities—believe school sex education classes are all a young person needs. Not true! Such classes are often just discussions of body functions and personal hygiene. What about moral values? Yes, today's children and teens often know all about bodily functions and sexual intercourse—they even have received a handbook on it—but have little knowledge of its effect on a young person's life. Teens and preteens will be instructed on how to use a condom and on the danger of AIDS. Many of them will gain the false impression that birth control makes sexual intercourse "safe" and harmless.

Statistics tell us nothing about our own child, of course. Yet surveyors report that more than one-third of teens have had sexual intercourse before their fifteenth birthday. So in any case, our child probably knows classmates who are sexually active. Adolescents may think of pregnancy or fathering a child as something that happens only to someone else—or only after prolonged periods of sexual intercourse. They may know the medical facts about abortion, but not the spiritual and psychological implications.

As responsible parents, we'll know the policy in our child's school—what's being presented to each grade. We'll remember that parents have the legal right to view books, handouts, videos, etc., and *we'll use it!* How else can we know what's being presented as "normal" and "acceptable"? How else can we communicate accurately with our child, to counter or to supplement information already acquired?

In Christian schools, the Learning about Sex series often is used in the classroom. Correlated materials for classroom use are available and may be previewed by parents and teachers.

They're Not Too Young to Know

And if we think our children are too young to hear such things at 11 or 12 or 13, we're only kidding ourselves. Youngsters that age—and younger—are engaging in sexual activity and becoming parents.

Also, if we haven't done so before, this is an excellent time to establish an open-door policy for our children's friends. Interaction with others is always helpful, and what better place for it than in our own home? Church youth groups usually offer opportunity for wholesome group participation.

"Phil and I have always dropped whatever we were doing to see that our kids got to the youth group activities at church. And we do whatever we can to help," remarked Patti. "The group isn't perfect, of course, but at least we know where our kids are and what they're hearing. Just to spend time with other Christian kids and to feel they are part of our church family has to be a good influence—and every little bit helps!"

Dealing with Self-stimulation—Again

Statistics tell us that most people of this age masturbate. Why do they do it? Simply because it's pleasurable—especially so now that the young person is experiencing newly developing sexual feelings. Part of the reason for masturbation, then, may be the desire to experiment, to discover more about one's burgeoning sexual development.

Recognizing that most young people overcome this habit as they mature, you'll want to be careful that you do not overreact. A harsh, shaming approach can do more harm than good—particularly if it becomes simply a matter of "laying down the law."

Young people may have heard the myths of dreadful consequences of self-stimulation. Or they might wonder whether they're some kind of "pervert."

So, you'll want to assure your young person that there is no evidence that self-stimulation causes any *physical* harm. However, young people need to realize that this quick release from sexual tension can become addictive (1 Corinthians 6:12). Persistent, compulsive masturbation can be the symptom of a deeper psychological and spiritual problem. The individual may withdraw, using self-stimulation as a way to cope with feelings of inadequacy, loneliness, rejection. It may also make it more difficult to learn how to relate to persons of the other sex, to deal with awkwardness, sexual tensions, and personal uncertainties inherent in adolescence. Sadly, self-stimulation can distort one's understanding of God's intent: the joy in marriage. For a future flesh-and-blood wife (or husband) will desire tenderness and touching and time, not just a quick "rush" that relieves. At any age, self-stimulation can only be a temporary escape. Loneliness and inner longings continue, unrelieved.

Thus it's important that we parents be sympathetic listeners, seeking first to understand the pain that underlies persistent masturbation. Chances are great that the Christian young person is already feeling shame and guilt, particularly about the sexual fantasies that usually go with masturbation. Our compassionate understanding will help our young person to surface the guilt—and to hear again the good news of God's forgiveness.

Tell Them about STDs? Very Definitely!

Many parents are surprised to learn that sexually transmitted diseases (STDs) are epidemic among young people, even in junior high. Nor is it confined to juvenile delinquents or young people from problem homes.

For example, the school nurse from a small Midwestern town described one case involving a 12-year-old girl with gonorrhea. She had interviewed the parents and the girl and found them to be a close, loving family with apparently high morals, living in a comfortable, middle class home—seemingly the ideal environment for raising children. Yet authorities had already uncovered 36 contacts relating to this one 12-year-old girl, and the investigation was not yet complete.

Coping with the Changes

As any parent knows, young people often seem to undergo a complete personality change. They may act amazingly adult at times and minutes later throw a temper tantrum like a three-year-old or revert to a whining, frightened child in need of comfort. Although trying, these abrupt mood swings are a normal part of the development process.

Youngsters may also seem determined to avoid as much contact with family members as possible. "When Lauren was 13, she became a sort of hermit around here," said Lisa. "I think she spent most of that year and part of the next up in her room! She'd come down for meals—reluctantly. Then just as surely as the sun rises in the east, one of us would inadvertently make some remark that would set her off. She'd dash for the stairs, slam every door loudly and vanish again. Honestly, none of us could say or do anything right!"

Lauren's behavior pattern was not unusual, and most youngsters pass through it on their own timetable.

Let Them Know They're Okay

Unfortunately, the child's grown-up look may make either or both parents uncomfortable. Parents may think they shouldn't touch their children anymore, that perhaps it's "wrong." Yet a hug, a pat on the back, positive assurances such as "You're really a nice person and I love you" are exactly what the developing adolescent needs. Such frequent, genuine gestures affirm our youngsters' feelings of acceptability as persons, in spite of their own nagging self-doubt.

Our adolescent children need our approval more than ever. Besides their own fears and insecurities, the climate in which young people operate is often one of continuing put-downs by their peers. Even good friends may think it's extremely clever to be sarcastic—especially since it usually brings a laugh—at someone else's expense. There are young people who are expert surgeons; they know each person's weak spot and just how to dissect another's ego.

Dealing with Labels

Another thing that many youngsters live with is the fear of being labeled homosexual. Some youngsters struggle with guilt feelings and uncertainty because of episodes of homosexual play. (Such behavior does occur, especially among young boys.) Also, males who are small for their age, who are slightly built or have a high-pitched voice, are often labeled as homosexual. A girl who appears boyish may be dubbed a "lez."

This effectively ensures that friends keep their distance, that young people try to act so there won't be any doubt about their sexual nature, perhaps purposely adopting a belligerent manner. But if their physical characteristics cast them into a mold, how can they escape? That's why it's important to reassure them that their bodies are developing according to their own individual timetables. If such a growth pattern is a family characteristic, or if a parent has had similar feelings, it helps them to hear of it.

For instance, when Craig saw his son moping around the house, refusing to go out and play ball with his friends, he suspected the reason. "You know, Eric, when I was your age, I had a terrible time. I was the runt of my class. The guys in my P.E. class acted like I had the plague or something. It seemed I could never throw a ball right or do anything else right, for that matter. And the girls, well, they totally ignored me. There I was, 14, and I looked about 10! Even when Grandpa told me that all the Meyer men had been built like me when they were my age, it didn't help one bit.

"But you know what? The year I was a junior in high school I grew a foot and put on 30 pounds."

Craig's remarks helped his son to accept his body—to feel okay about himself. But there's the opposite problem, too; there's the girl who develops earlier than her contemporaries and is "really built." Such a girl has her own difficulties, for she is almost inevitably labeled "hot." The boys make suggestive remarks, and the other girls (who are envious and on different timetables) spin wild tales. And although it happens less frequently, an early developing boy can experience similar problems.

Comparisons Can Be Harmful

Although parents can be helpful, as Craig was, they can also damage their children's self-image through thoughtless remarks and constant comparisons with others. "My mom had one strategy when I was growing up—and I hated it!" said Mindy. "When my friends were around, she'd say something like, 'Mindy, when are you going to stop being so clumsy?' or 'Don't go into Mindy's room—it looks like a pigpen!' My friends would laugh, but I'd be dying inside.

"Or she'd praise my sister, who was a brain, and ask, 'Why can't you be more like Stephanie? You're just as smart as she is. Obviously, you just don't study as hard.' Teachers said the same thing, year after year.

"But if the plan was to make me work harder, it backfired. I just resented all of them—Mom for ridiculing and nagging me all the time and poor Steph for her good grades. And I hated myself most of all, because I saw myself as a loser who would never measure up."

A far better course of action is when we frequently tell our children it's okay to be different—that in fact we rejoice in their individuality and they should, too. If we can instill in them the solid conviction that God made them as they are, that there never has been nor ever will be another person just like them—that God has a plan for using their strengths and weaknesses, many potential problems of later life will never appear.

A Climate for Growth

Establishing an atmosphere where we can speak comfortably about sexual concerns will help our children know they are free to come to us for advice and answers. Surely that's what we want, isn't it, even if it makes us a bit uneasy at times?

All this is part of raising children to become well-adjusted adults. One psychologist says, "Wise parents work themselves out of a job." Our goal is young adults who have a God-pleasing set of values, healthy attitudes, and the ability to govern themselves.

There are times when that seems an impossible task, because we're well aware of our failures and weaknesses. We can't do it on our own! So we pray for God's guidance and forgiveness, and we trust Him to use even our mistakes.

—————— **Questions Parents Ask** ——————

R- and NC-17-Rated Entertainment

Help! My kids say I don't want them to have any fun because I set limits on their time in front of the TV, and strictly limit movies. They say they know it's not real life, so what difference does it make? I'm tired of the struggle!

Parents today face challenges on all sides. Videos, cable and satellite TV, and computer networks greatly multiply the array of erotic and even pornographic images being beamed into our homes. It's difficult enough for scrupulous parents to limit such exposure at home, but nearly impossible when children visit friends.

The rating system for movies and videos is imperfect at best. Check reviews in parenting magazines you trust, or preview them yourself. Pool information with reliable friends. Investigate the variety of blocking devices or services available from manufacturers and through cable TV companies, either directly or by referral. Absolute control of television viewing is possible.

Unfortunately, it doesn't stop with television and movies. You may be unaware what's offered via computer networks. For example, when users log on to many networks, available options often include bulletin boards or chat rooms. They provide an easy route for pedophiles and other criminal types to obtain personal information, as documented by law enforcement agencies. Some networks offer lines where users can "talk dirty." The dazzling capabilities of state-of-the-art equipment and services make it possible for the computer-literate (of any age) to access what most of us would label "porn." Moving images, sound, and color combine into a form even children can view, over and over again.

Beware of being lulled by available blocking devices for computers hooked up to the Internet. Sexually explicit materials are *not* safely locked away in separate, labeled sections! They can be sprinkled throughout otherwise reliable categories of reference materials helpful for research. If our daughter or son is spending hours at the computer, it our responsibility to know what they're tapping into.

Even computer games pose a threat. Do you *know* what's on the screen when your child plays computer games or heads for the video arcade? Many of those games have a dark side, and some are incredibly violent. (Some have two versions: one "G-rated," the other featuring decapitation, squirting blood, etc.) Play them yourself, then make your own judgment of how many hours you want your child to spend riveted to the computer.

But don't just issue edicts. Talk it over with your child, explaining why you object to a particular movie or television program. Talk about your values as a Christian family. Don't moralize and lecture. Once your youngster is old enough to date or drive, of course, you'll have less control.

Yes, watching R-rated movies and suggestive or violent TV programming can influence young people. Studies show that heavy viewers of television and movies, both children and adults, tend to be more fearful about life in general. They also more readily accept abnormal behavior and deviant lifestyles as the norm. In other words, they begin to perceive life as portrayed on the screen or the tube rather than as it's lived by the average person.

We're all influenced by what we watch and read. It's a bit like that computer slogan—GIGO. That translates to "garbage in—garbage out." If true of computers, it's also true of the human mind.

Menstruation

My daughter and I talked about menstruation a couple of years ago. The school nurse also talked to the class about sex and menstruation at least once. Isn't that enough?

You've already spoken with your daughter. Good for you! But now she's older and able to understand a more detailed explanation. Besides, unless your daughter attends a Christian school, she'll know all about the "plumbing," but probably little or nothing about morality. Preteens need to hear their parents' perspective. (Even though your adolescent may tell you that you're out-of-date, you still are the number one authority. Count on it!)

If you want some printed back-up material, the menstrual process is described in Book 3 of this series, *How You Are Changing*, by Jane Graver. You will find this book very helpful. The companies that manufacture sanitary pads also have excellent illustrated booklets available. In any case, don't wait for your daughter to ask. Pick a time when you think you're communicating well on other levels, and then just begin.

You may wish to say something like this: "You're growing up fast, and soon you'll be an adult. Your body will go through many changes—changes that will prepare you to be an adult and to be a mother someday if you want to. One of the earliest signs may come when you notice a thick, white discharge on your panties. That means your body is maturing and getting ready for menstruation (men-strooway-shun). Most healthy girls menstruate. Some begin when they're about your age, a few earlier, and some much later. Some may begin as late as 18. No one knows exactly when a girl will have her first menstrual period.

"You have seen ads for feminine protection products on television. (Name some currently being advertised.) Those products are for a woman when she is having her menstrual period.

"It all begins with a part of your body called the pituitary gland. That gland controls your personal timetable. You may notice soon that you or some of your girlfriends are beginning to get hair under the arms and between the legs. Your breasts may begin to swell, and your waist will narrow down. These are all signs that your body is getting ready for you to become an adult woman.

"God designed females to have all the equipment they need to be a woman: two ovaries, two fallopian tubes, a uterus, and a vagina. (Show diagram if possible.) Your ovaries are filled with thousands of ova (also known as egg cells), which are the female reproductive cells. Those cells make it possible for you to have a baby someday if you choose.

"One day, when the pituitary gland signals that your body is ready, hormones will travel to your ovaries and tell them to get started doing their job. In about two weeks an egg cell leaves the ovary (called ovulation) and new hormones are secreted. These cause the blood and cells inside the walls of the uterus to swell.

"If the egg is fertilized by a sperm (the male cell), this rich new lining will provide a good place for the egg to fasten and begin to grow into a baby. Most of the time, though, the egg is not fertilized, and the uterus gets rid of this lining of old blood and cells.

"So your body must clean house. The old blood and cells from the uterus must leave the body. This is called the menstrual flow. It comes out through the natural passageway God designed—the vagina. The menstrual flow continues for about three to five days, and then it's all over for another month until your ovaries release another egg. Once it starts, your body will continue this regular cycle over and over for about 40 years, unless you become pregnant or ill.

"For most girls, menstrual periods are not painful. Most girls can go on doing everything they always do. Some girls get a little twinge or a slight cramp in their abdomen once in a while, but doctors say the best thing to do for that is to get some exercise—whatever you enjoy doing at other times.

"One of these days you'll go to the bathroom and you'll notice blood on the toilet paper or on your panties. That's like your body announcing to you that it's getting ready to be a grown-up body. If it happens at school, you can ask the school nurse or your (female) teacher for a sanitary pad. If you're in a public restroom, you may see a dispenser on the wall where you can drop in a coin and buy a sanitary pad. Of course, if it happens here at home you can come to me.

"Here, I'll show you how to use a sanitary pad so you'll know what to do. And I've bought you your own box to keep on your closet shelf, just in case I'm not here when you need them.

"In the beginning your periods may be irregular. After a while they will usually come about every 28 to 30 days. It's a good idea to mark your calendar on the first day of your period so you can keep track. Then you'll remember to take a pad with you in case you start your period away from home.

"You'll also learn quickly how often you need to change your sanitary pad. Other than changing your pad regularly, the only thing to remember is to bathe or shower often so that you feel fresh and clean."

Note to Mothers

Remember (again) that more is caught than taught. If your daughter observes you displaying negative attitudes during your own menstrual period—if you call menstruation "the curse," etc.—she will absorb and adopt the same attitude.

Be positive when you talk with your daughter. Once her periods have begun, casually ask whether she has any questions. Some girls do experience severe cramping. Be ready to deal with it, but don't suggest it. If you notice her discomfort, begin with the obvious—standard pain medication such as aspirin or acetaminophen. (If these are insufficient, your doctor could prescribe a form that includes codeine.) Another over-the-counter medication, ibuprofen, has proven effective for painful menses in some females. (See section on PMS in chapter 7 for additional information.)

How old should a girl be before she begins to use a tampon? What about toxic shock syndrome?

If a girl has been menstruating for six months or more and her body is normal, she should have no trouble using a tampon. Explain that the tampon is a pack of absorbent cotton or gauze attached to a string, which is inserted into the vagina to absorb the menstrual flow. Assure her that no harm comes from inserting a tampon into the vagina and that it is not painful—unless she is nervous or frightened and thus tightens the muscles at the vaginal entrance. If a girl has a good attitude and remains relaxed, a little practice should make insertion and removal simple. Most brands pack an instruction leaflet in each box.

Toxic shock syndrome (TSS) made the news some years back. Although TSS has been reported in males and females, most cases were tampon-related. Authorities found that the use of a particular brand of high-absorbency tampon (now off the market) was involved in the majority of cases. Today most physicians consider tampon usage safe, particularly the less-absorbent tampons.

Impress upon your daughter that tampons are *not* to be left in place all day long, even on days when menstrual flow is light. Change tampons at least every six to eight hours. Some doctors advise the use of sanitary napkins at night and tampons only during the day.

Should boys be told about menstruation?

Yes, boys should be given the same basic information at about the same age. In particular, emphasize that the menstrual cycle is a normal and natural part of the female life. It's also good for a boy to understand that if a girl declines sports activity or the like, he should accept her decision without expecting a long explanation.

Explaining the Gynecological Exam

My adolescent daughter is due for a complete physical exam. I remember how embarrassed and frightened I was the first time I had a gynecological checkup. How can I prepare my daughter?

Talk it through with your daughter so she knows what to expect. You may wish to say something like this: "Now that you're growing up, the doctor needs to check and make sure that your body is developing normally. So he may want to do a vaginal examination. He'll tell you to take your panties off and to cover yourself with a large cloth. Or perhaps he may tell you to take off all your clothes and put on a gown. Either way, he'll leave the examining room while you're changing clothes, but the nurse may help you.

"When he comes back in, he should check your breasts, too. This is an important part of a regular exam for a female, just to make sure everything is okay. He will give you literature on self breast examination and explain the procedure. Next he or the nurse will tell you to put your feet into the holders on the sides of the table and to scoot down. You'll be covered with a sheet, but you'll probably think the whole thing must look pretty ridiculous with your knees sticking up in the air. And you'll be right, because it is rather undignified! But it makes it easier for the doctor to examine you.

"Next the doctor may move a light closer, and he'll most likely insert a metal instrument into your vagina. It might feel cold and you may feel a little pressure. The doctor uses the instrument to spread the lips of the vagina apart so that he can see more easily. He'll look inside, and he may also insert a finger (he'll be wearing rubber gloves) so that he can feel if everything is as it should be. He may also press on your stomach sometime during the examination.

"The doctor will also want to do a Pap smear test, so he'll take a long cotton swab and get a sample of the cells present in the cervix (mouth of the uterus). This will be smeared on a piece of glass and sent to a laboratory for examination. Now that you're growing up, you'll have regular Pap tests, because it's an important way to make sure that everything is normal.

"That's usually all there is to it. It would be a lot easier, of course, if a female's reproductive system weren't all inside the body, but that's the way God made us. Getting a gynecological exam is a routine thing for women of all ages. It doesn't hurt, so just try to be relaxed.

"Perhaps you're wondering what the doctor thinks about all this. Well, doctors see all parts of the body all day, every day, day after day. When they examine a female, they're just looking for signs of problems and checking for the way various membranes look and that sort of thing. They are not touching the female in a sexual way; it's just part of their responsibility to help people stay well.

"Like any other new experience, having an exam may make you feel a bit self-conscious or embarrassed, soon you'll feel at ease about it. And all of us need to take good care of these marvelous bodies God gave us. The vagina and uterus are very important parts of our body, and we want to do everything we can to keep them healthy. And always remember: You are the physician's patient, and you should feel free to ask questions not only then but at any time you need help in clarifying physical problems."

Note to Mothers

Usually annual examinations are unnecessary for young women in good health until they reach their late teens or early twenties. However, if your daughter has problems with menstruation or questions about her reproductive organs, or if she's sexually active or considering marriage, an exam is called for.

A young girl may be uncomfortable if left alone in the examining room with a male doctor. You have a right to remain in the room with your daughter if she prefers. Or she may want to have only a female nurse present. Either way, make sure your daughter knows she can make her requests known. If necessary, you take the initiative and insist upon it so this exam turns out to be a positive experience for her.

Nocturnal Emissions

How should a boy be prepared for nocturnal emissions (wet dreams)?

A casual explanation of nocturnal emissions (preferably by the father or other close male—simply because he speaks from firsthand knowledge) should be given at about age 12, before they begin. If a mother has an open relationship with her son and feels comfortable talking with him about sexual matters, she can do the honors.

The son should be told that while he is dreaming—perhaps about girls—his penis may stiffen, allowing the urethra to straighten out. Then the semen, containing sperm, shoots out (ejaculation). There is no "normal" interval between wet dreams; for some boys it is days, for some weeks.

If a boy is not prepared in advance, the first time he wakes up and finds a whitish, sticky material on his pajamas or the sheets he may be totally bewildered. The color and consistency will tell him it's not urine—but what is it? He may be mortified and wonder what his mother will think when she washes his sheets. He may even think he is sick in some way.

Reassure him that this is a normal, healthy sign that his body is maturing, that he's getting ready to be a man. Also, either in this discussion or at another time, you'll want to point out that wet dreams are a sign he is physically able to father a child, although he is far from ready to be a father, with all that entails.

Don't be alarmed and assume that nocturnal emissions (no matter how frequent) mean your son is obsessed with sex. These occur during the dream state and are a natural way of draining off sexual tensions. Don't question him or ask what kind of dreams he had or make a big deal out of it in any way. Wet dreams are as natural for boys as menstruation is for girls.

(Normal adult men may also have nocturnal emissions, especially during times of prolonged abstinence.)

Should I explain nocturnal emissions to my daughter?

Yes, explain the process and caution her not to taunt her brother(s). Also emphasize that this is the male body's built-in method for taking care of sexual tensions. Therefore, if a young man ever confronts your daughter with the argument that he must have intercourse or "he'll go crazy," she'll be aware that this is not true.

Talking to Preteens about Their Bodies

I told my children the facts of life long ago. Now that they are ages 10 and 12, how much more should I say?

When talking to your 10- to 14-year-old about sex, present the basic general facts but personalize them to fit. You may wish to say something like this: "We've talked about sex before, but now that you're older you'll look at it differently than you did before. Besides, you may have forgotten some of the terms, so let's go over it again.

"Here's a drawing of the body parts of the male body and the female body. (Show them the diagrams on pages 138–140 of this book or those in *Love, Sex, and God,* Book 5 in this series.) You know that the male sexual organ is called the penis. Males also pass urine through the penis. The body takes what it needs to stay healthy from the food we eat, then collects the wastes for elimination. The liquid waste, called urine, is collected in the bladder and passes out through the urethra, which is a hollow tube somewhat like a soda straw. A male's urethra is in his penis. A female's urethra is inside her body, and there's a small opening on the outside.

"A male also has testicles—two egg-shaped bodies that manufacture sperm. The sperm are male reproductive cells so tiny you need a microscope to see them. At your age a male's body is maturing so that he can father children. Sometimes he is puzzled when his penis suddenly gets stiff. This is called an erection. It sticks out, and he may feel embarrassed about it.

"Some boys find their breasts swelling a bit, and they may think they'll end up looking like a girl. But they won't—it's only a temporary thing and nothing to get self-conscious about. Sometimes a boy's nipples get hard, too. All these are signs that his body is getting ready for the day when he'll be ready to marry and perhaps have children.

"Because normal body temperature would destroy the sperm, God designed the testicles to be outside the body, inside a pouch of skin called the scrotum, where the temperature is a couple of degrees cooler. If a fellow should happen to bump his testicles or get kicked there when playing football, it would probably hurt a lot because there are many nerve endings concentrated there. That's why it's a good idea to protect the testicles and penis from injury.

"You can see by the diagram that a female's reproductive system is all up inside her body." (When talking to a young girl, it's well to add: "You might be curious to see what your own body looks like. It's not easy to look at yourself without a mirror. Sometime when you're alone, you might want to compare your own body with the diagram so you'll know the names for the parts of your body." Young girls sometimes think "nice girls" don't look at themselves. Your suggestion will let her know it's okay.) "A female has two egg-shaped parts, too, called the ovaries. This is where the ova, or egg cells, are stored. Every girl is on her own timetable, so there's no exact age when it happens, but one day one of her ovaries will release an egg, which will travel down the fallopian tubes to the uterus.

"The uterus has been getting ready for the egg, building up a thick lining of rich blood cells to nourish it, in case the egg cell has been joined by a male sperm, which we call fertilization. Most of the time it hasn't, so after a couple of weeks the unused blood cells just loosen and become the girl's monthly menstrual flow.

"If the egg cell had been fertilized, a baby would begin to grow in the uterus. At your age a girl's body is just going through the menstrual cycle to get ready for the day when she's ready for marriage and may want to have a baby. But once a girl begins to menstruate, it's possible for her to have a baby.

"Your body is growing and changing in many ways. You'll notice as you look at your friends that they come in all shapes and sizes. Some are short, some are tall. Some are fat, some are thin. Boys have penises and testicles that are different shapes and sizes, too. ([Matt], perhaps you've wondered whether your penis is 'normal' size.) You've probably noticed that girls come in all shapes and sizes. ([Erica], you may have worried that you're too flat in front—or too round in back.) Some girls your age have been menstruating for a while, yet others haven't even begun. But you need to know one thing for sure: God made each of us an individual, and that means we have our own schedule for growing up, too.

"You're also growing hair under your arms and between your legs—what's called the pubic area. Some people have a lot of pubic hair, others not much. It's meant as a protection for your sex organs and also to keep your skin from getting irritated by perspiration.

"And I've seen you frowning into the mirror at your zits (acne). These are normal, too. All these changes are happening because your hormone balance is changing from a child's to that of an adult. It takes a while to get everything balanced perfectly, so there will be times when your zits will be worse. Your skin and hair are more oily, too, and you probably perspire more.

"All this is okay! Remember this: Each person is on a different schedule, so each one is normal for him or her. Wouldn't it be boring if we were all alike? There's never any need to worry, nor should you ever make fun of anyone else. It's all part of God's wonderful design when He made us male and female.

Explaining Sexual Intercourse

I guess I need to talk about intercourse with my daughter, but I'm really self-conscious about it! I suspect that when I talk about "the man" and "the woman," she'll picture my husband and me in action. Besides, I think she already knows more than I did when I got married! Why should I embarrass us both?

Many other parents would say the same thing. True, today's young people pick up visual images and familiarity with the topic of sex from entertainment media. School sex education classes expose youngsters to medical data and facts on reproduction. But who will help them understand relationships? It's up to parents to set all this in a godly context. If not you, then who will do it?

It's natural to feel awkward when discussing sexual intercourse with our children. Don't let that stop you, even if you stumble over the words. Underneath your adolescent's veneer of sophistication lurks a lot of faulty information.

As you contemplate beginning this discussion, remember that this is the same child you've known and loved all these years. According to knowledgeable researchers, most teenagers still list their parents as the authority they count on. (Few would admit that to parents, of course.) When you broach the subject of sex, most likely you'll hear giggles or groans of protest; perhaps you'll both blush a few times. This oh-so-cool young person may appear to tune you out but will be listening intently, nevertheless. So fix your purpose in mind and forge ahead.

You may wish to say something like this, again personalizing it to fit:

"You're old enough now that sometimes you may experience some exciting, confusing emotions. Maybe you've been around a boy (girl) and suddenly your heart was pounding or your stomach felt quivery. You wanted to say something funny or clever, but your brain seemed to have left your head. Besides, your mouth was so dry you wouldn't have been able to get the words out. Probably you wondered, 'What's going on, anyhow?'

"Those feelings are part of what we call 'sexual attraction.' Believe it or not, those very emotions are part of God's gift to His people— His precious gift of sexuality. You've probably studied enough about animals to know that they mate and reproduce by instinct. It's as if they can't help themselves.

"But it's not like that with human males and females, because God endowed us with brains and emotions. God *gifted* us human beings with our sexual nature. Genesis 1 says He created us, male and female, in His own image! God wants us to *enjoy* His wonderful gift.

"You see, Honey, God brought that first male and female together in marriage, and the Bible says that Adam and Eve were united in one flesh. That's a good description, because the closest physical relationship any man and woman can have is sexual intercourse."

Don't Settle for Less!

You probably have a good illustration of your own to explain the specialness of the physical relationship between husband and wife. If not, maybe this story will do:

"It's not exaggerating to say that God's gift of sexuality is like a precious gemstone. We live in a society full of imitations that *look* so real they could fool us. Lots of people don't know the difference between the genuine and the counterfeit.

"Let's just suppose that I buy a beautiful ring for $3,000, believing that I have a valuable, perfect diamond. I show my 'diamond' to everyone I know, and I tell them how happy I am to have it. Maybe after a few months or years I get tired of it, or I spot an emerald that I like even more. So I decide to sell the diamond, then use the money to buy the emerald.

"I take the ring to a fine jeweler and I say, 'I spent my savings of $3,000 to buy this diamond not long ago. I've enjoyed owning it, and now I want to sell it. I'd like a written appraisal that reflects the ring's true value.'

"Imagine how shocked I'd be if the jeweler replied, 'This stone is only an imitation of the real thing. This ring is very pretty, and I'm sure it has brought you much pleasure. But actually it is only worthless costume jewelry. I'm sorry to tell you that you wasted your inheritance on this poor imitation of a valuable diamond.'

"What a disappointment that would be! My money would be gone. I'm not rich. Perhaps I could never accumulate another spare $3,000. I'd feel that I'd wasted my savings on a worthless bauble. And I'd probably begin to wonder whether there's anybody or anything I could trust.

"It's too bad, but that's exactly the way many people live their lives. By engaging is sex outside the security of marriage, they settle for a poor imitation of God's very best. God knows that growing a happy, fulfilling sexual relationship takes time. So He planned for sex to only take place within a marriage. In marriage the husband and wife pledge their lives to each other, and they promise to be faithful to each other. When they come together—when they become one flesh—they give their bodies to each other as a priceless marriage gift.

The Freedom of Marriage

"Think about it. Both marriage partners can relax, unhurried and secure in their relationship. There are no worries about any diseases they might have picked up from previous sexual encounters or children from previous sexual relationships. The wife and the husband have the rest of their lives to grow in love and to work out any adjustments that are needed.

"If the wife becomes pregnant—and remember that can happen any time a male and a female have intercourse, even when they use birth control—the couple already has a home for their child. Their baby will be born to *two* parents who are ready to welcome and to love their little daughter or son.

"You're old enough to know that some marriages break up, and there can be many reasons why. Sadly, some marriage partners are unfaithful and don't live up to their promises. Sometimes the bride or groom may already have one or more children, and the new family doesn't get along. Or there may be an ex-spouse or ex-boyfriend or girlfriend who causes trouble. Eventually the couple separates.

"Can such people ever reconcile and live a satisfying life? Yes. God specializes in new beginnings, you know. But if you ask any of them, I'm sure they'd tell you that their life would be less complicated if they had followed God's plan for one woman and one man to marry for life and be faithful for life.

Just the Basics …

"Maybe you're wondering whether marriage partners have intercourse only when they want to make a baby. The answer is no. From time to time the husband and wife feel extra-loving. They want to touch each other—all over—in this extra-special way. When they have these feelings about each other, the husband's penis begins to get hard and straight. The wife's vagina gets ready for intercourse, too, by becoming softer and more relaxed and lubricated by vaginal secretions.

"As they lie close to each other, the husband puts his penis into the wife's vagina, in just the way God planned. They begin to move their bodies together, enjoying the pleasurable feelings it gives them. Soon the testicles release some sperm and the seminal fluid comes out through the penis and into the wife's vagina. This does not hurt the wife in any way. The name for this is ejaculation, and you should know that urine never comes out at the same time as the semen. After ejaculation the penis becomes smaller and softer.

"The wife doesn't ejaculate, of course. But she has the same good feelings as her husband. When sexual intercourse is over, the husband and wife enjoy the way they feel—warm and relaxed and very, very loving.

"A husband and wife enjoy having intercourse very much. Sooner or later they may want to have a baby, and this also begins with intercourse and the union of the egg cell and the sperm. During ejaculation millions of sperm are released. The sperm are shaped like tiny commas, and they swim rapidly toward the fallopian tubes, trying to get to the egg cell, which is smaller than a dot. As soon as one has penetrated the tiny egg, no more sperm can penetrate it, and pregnancy has begun.

"Now the fertilized egg moves from the fallopian tube to the uterus. It attaches itself to the inside of the uterus. Remember when we talked about the rich lining of tissue containing many blood vessels that the uterus prepares each month? Well, those blood cells nourish the egg and help it get off to a good start. Within a very short time this one cell—the union of sperm and egg—will begin to divide and form two cells. The two divide into four and so on. This tiny cell is the beginning of a baby that will grow inside the woman's uterus. This is how you and I and everyone else on earth got here, and it's part of God's wonderful plan for men and women.

"Pretty soon you may think you're grown-up and ready to have sexual intercourse, even to have a baby. Perhaps some of your friends are even bragging about having sex. Some teens even tell themselves that if they make a baby they become "a real man" or "a real woman." But they're not thinking straight. Are teenagers really ready to care for a baby, 24 hours a day? Are they prepared to be patient if their baby cries all day and doesn't sleep at night? Are they set to stay home and not complain, ready to give up running around with their friends? Can they make a home and pay their bills?

"God means for a baby to be born to two parents who have promised to live their whole lives together in marriage. Two parents who will love their baby and care for it and together, watch their child grow up. Oh sure, teenagers do make babies. But they're not equipped to make a good life for years! People who accept less than God's best—like some of the characters on television or in the movies, who have intercourse with first one person and then another—are missing out on the best. They're settling for second-rate. And many times they mess up their whole lives."

Telling Youngsters about Pregnancy and Birth

How much do I tell my preteen about pregnancy and birth?

Youngsters this age are extremely curious about this subject. They want to know everything. Blessed indeed is the adolescent who can talk freely with understanding parents.

Answer questions honestly, calmly and casually, so your youngster absorbs the idea that this is a natural part of living. If you're stumped, admit it and promise to find the answer. Then do it.

Also, don't read great significance into the questions asked. A chance remark or something in the media may have aroused curiosity. Beware of pouncing with a WHY-do-you-want-to-know? attitude or you'll not get a second chance to have your child talk freely with you.

It's assumed your youngster knows the names of body parts and functions from previous conversations. However, it can be helpful to refer to a diagram of the human body and briefly review. Then you can be sure your child will understand the terminology.

You may wish to say something like this: "Sometimes a husband and wife may decide they want to have a baby. And we've talked before about how the egg cell from the wife and the sperm from the husband unite in the fallopian tube of the female. We say the egg cell has been fertilized by the sperm. This is the beginning of new life. This new cell then travels to the uterus (also called the womb) and begins to grow.

"Hair color, eye color, the shape of the nose and the mouth—all these and a bunch of other qualities, including the baby's sex, are determined at the instant of conception. Isn't that marvelous? Each new child is unique—a special person, with special talents and abilities. There never has been—and never will be—another human being just like you.

"After conception that tiny clump of new life fastens onto the inside of the female's uterus, which has been prepared with a soft, thick cushion of tissue with many small blood vessels filled with lots of rich, red blood cells to nourish the growing child. The mother's first hint that she's pregnant comes when she misses her regular menstrual period. After that there are special tests to make sure.

"The developing new life is called the embryo. Soon it's surrounded by fluid and enclosed in a membrane. What keeps the embryo alive and makes it grow? Well, it's attached to the wall of the uterus and gets its food and oxygen right from its mother's bloodstream. Wastes are eliminated in the same way. That means that when a pregnant woman eats a good diet, the baby gets proper nourishment, too. But if she does something harmful—if she takes drugs or drinks alcohol or eats poorly or smokes cigarettes—the baby takes in the same thing and may be harmed. For instance, it may not develop properly.

"The embryo—that bit of new life from the mother and the father—keeps growing and developing. While the woman is pregnant, the doctor may perform an ultrasound (sonogram)—a test that's painless for the mother and harmless to the embryo. Just four weeks after the egg is fertilized the doctor can see the baby's tiny body in its membrane sac! By five weeks after fertilization, the doctor can see the baby's heart beat! After the eighth week, it's called a fetus. By the fourth or fifth month, the doctor can hear the baby's heartbeat with his stethoscope and the mother can feel the baby moving and kicking.

"The baby continues to grow in the uterus for about nine months. Then when it is ready to be born, the woman begins to feel labor pains. Usually labor begins as a kind of cramping in the lower abdomen, accompanied by a feeling of tightness in the lower back. Soon these contractions begin to come at regular times as her body gets ready for the baby's birth. The opening to the uterus, called the cervix, is stretching to allow the baby to come out. The contractions get closer and closer together. The mother usually has a doctor or midwife there to help her with the birth, and most of the time she goes to the hospital when labor begins. Perhaps you're wondering whether it hurts for the mother's body to stretch like that. Most mothers have some pain, but if you ask them they usually say they didn't really mind because they knew the discomfort was accomplishing something. It was bringing their new baby into the world! It's a bit like when you're sore after running in a track meet; you don't mind the aching muscles because it was worth it to win the prize.

"The birth process is called delivery, and it may take several hours before the cervix has stretched enough to allow the baby to pass into the birth canal or vagina. But it's not as bad as it sounds because in between contractions the mother can just relax and she feels quite comfortable. Finally the baby is ready to make its appearance. The opening of the vagina must also stretch, and although you might think it couldn't possibly enlarge enough to allow a baby to pass through, you'd be wrong, because that's exactly what happens.

"And so the baby is born, with the umbilical cord still attached. Once the infant takes its first breath and its lungs inflate, the cord is not needed anymore, so it's cut and clamped—which doesn't hurt the baby. (Your navel or belly button shows where the umbilical cord used to be.) The child is then laid on the mother's breast so she can see and touch this little person she's been waiting for. The placenta and the sac that surrounded the baby come out of the vagina last, and then the mother's uterus and vaginal opening begin to get smaller. Soon they have returned almost to the exact size they were before she became pregnant.

"I remember how it was when you were born. We looked at you and were amazed that God could take that tiny bit from each of us and form it into you. You were God's gift to us. And we were very thankful that He watched over all of us.

"Like all new parents, we looked you over very carefully. And we marveled that you could be a real, separate, living person—that you had blood vessels and a heart, lungs that could breathe, and a voice that could yell surprisingly loud! That reminded us of Psalm 139:13, 15–16, where it says:

> *You created every part of me; You put me together in my*
> *mother's womb ... When my bones were being formed, ...*
> *when I was growing there in secret, You knew that I was*
> *there—You saw me before I was born (TEV).*

"It really is a miracle from God, isn't it? But there's another miracle, too. After the baby's birth, the mother's breasts begin to fill with milk. The baby is born with the instinct to suck, so it knows what to do. And usually a mother has just enough milk for her own baby. As the child grows bigger and drinks more milk, the mother's breasts produce a larger supply. If she had twins, she would have enough milk for them, too. You might say the supply equals the demand.

"Are you wondering whether it hurts the mother when the baby nurses? The answer is no. Sometimes for the first few days her breasts may be a bit tender. But a mother feels so good that she can give her child what's needed that the tiny bit of discomfort doesn't bother her. After a week or two, both she and the baby feel like old pros. Later, when the baby gets older, the mother may decide it's time to start giving milk from a cup or a bottle. And then her breasts stop producing milk and get smaller, as they were before she got pregnant.

"You may notice that some mothers always feed their babies from a bottle. But they hold their babies close and love them just as much as the mothers who breast-feed, and the babies are healthy, too. It all depends on what the parents and the doctor think is best.

"You're old enough to know that sometimes people have babies under other circumstances, such as when a teenage girl isn't married and has a child. Such a mother may still love her child, but it's much harder because she feels all alone. And God really meant for children to be born and to live in families, where there are parents who are able to support themselves and care for the children.

"Of course, there are all kinds of families. Some homes may have just a mother, some just a father. Maybe one parent has died or the parents have been divorced. That doesn't mean kids can't be happy in such a home. It just means the parent has to work harder at the job and everybody in the family has to pull together even more. Because that's what a family is—people who love each other and care about each other and help each other."

Rape

Is date rape really a danger, or is it just media hype? When should I bring it up with my kids?

This is prime time for the young person to establish personal standards for friendships. "Acquaintance rape" ("date rape") is forced, unwanted intercourse with someone known to the victim. (Most rapes are *not* committed by strangers.) So it's vital that we discuss the subject with daughters—and sons. You may want to introduce some guidelines for dating, and in that context tie in the subject of acquaintance rape.

Your goal is common-sense caution, not fear. Young people need to realize that many elements are in their control, if they think ahead. Sexual attraction between healthy young people always has been— always will be—dangerous. Even well-balanced, sound-judgment teens "forget," and live to regret their impulsiveness. Our society's over-emphasis on sex intensifies the awareness and concentration on sex.

Because females are the principle targets for rape, they would do well to keep in mind the points listed below. Young males need to look at the same points and consider how *they* respond. Here's a partial list of practical issues to talk through:

- Choose your companions carefully. Females need to know the males with whom they spend time. (As a parent, it's good for you to insist that you meet them, even though your daughter may protest.)
- *Always* trust your own feelings. If you're uneasy, walk away! If a situation somehow doesn't "feel right," get out of there. If an individual makes you feel uncomfortable, leave. Never allow someone

to embarrass you into sticking around. *You don't need a reason to leave!*

- Smart girls don't get into a car full of boys, especially at night.
- *Nobody* should ride with people who've been drinking. Good judgment and self-control dissolve in the booze. And you can't predict how another person will behave when intoxicated.
- Avoid risky situations and locations. Willingly accompanying a companion can signal "implied consent," especially if you'll be alone and isolated. (Counselors report that today's most common setting for teenage sexual activity is the home, usually when parents are away.)
- Be clear about your own sexual standards, and make them known early in the relationship. If a boy protests or seems not to hear, the girl should not stay with him.
- Don't send mixed messages. Say yes only when you mean it, and be sure that your no means no. (For example, sexual remarks, teasing, fondling, and dress can be interpreted as a *yes* signal, despite the word *no*.)
- Alcohol and drugs impair judgment, your own and your date's.
- Never assume that you and your date can go "so far and no farther." Hormones can replace good judgment pretty quickly, especially for young men.
- The ancient line, "If you really loved me ..." reveals that the speaker loves no one but himself (herself).
- It's never right to pressure or force oneself on another person.
- Sexual excitement is no excuse; each of us is responsible for our actions.
- Boys do well to live by these same standards. It's no longer rare for a young man to be accused of rape, even though he had assumed there was mutual consent. Some have been wrongly accused, even convicted. Wise individuals (of either sex) who avoid compromising situations prove more convincing in their own defense.

Be sure that you wind up your discussion with solid reassurance. For as Christians we have reason to celebrate, at any age! Christ living in us is greater than any situation we may encounter (see 1 John 4:4; 1 Corinthians 10:13). Certainly He promises to help Christian young people resolved to use their precious gift of sexuality wisely.

What about the danger of rape from a stranger?

Certainly females young and old fear such attack. There are precautions that lessen the danger. First, impress on your daughter that rape by a stranger is *not*, as most people think, related to sex alone. It includes a large component of violence and rage. The rapist wants to act out his hate. A female, being physically weaker, becomes the "logical" target.

Because of this growing problem, most major cities now have rape crisis centers where victims can get sympathetic medical care and counseling. Females should be encouraged to contact this service in case of need—before they do anything else, such as take a shower or change clothes.

All of us—women and men alike—must stop associating shame with the victim of rape. The shame and guilt should rest on the rapist, not the victim. For in spite of all the old jokes, an attacker who holds a switchblade or who threatens with a gun, who is bigger and physically stronger—and powerfully determined as well—can force a female to submit. At that moment she can't be sure the sick-minded man who promises to slit her throat is not serious. For most victims, submitting is equated with simple survival.

We should warn even our young daughter about being cautious and teach her some simple safety guidelines. (Contact your local public library, police station, or rape crisis center for more information.) But it's important to keep a balanced perspective. We don't want her to fear every male she sees. Our goal should rather be a healthy respect for hazardous situations and an attitude of sensible caution. And we'll want to emphasize again and again that our daughter can tell us *anything*.

By the way, occasionally a male is raped by a bigger, stronger male. As with the rape of a female, this is a power trip for the rapist.

Transvestites and Transsexuals

My kids saw something on television the other day and asked me all about transvestites and transsexuals. Help!

By definition, a transvestite derives sexual pleasure from dressing in clothes of the opposite sex. A transsexual identifies with the opposite sex, sometimes even undergoing sex-change surgery. In either case, most are males and are not homosexuals. Television shows notwithstanding, these individuals represent a *small* segment of society.

Transvestites do not wish to take hormones or to change their sex. Usually they have normal heterosexual relationships, often are married, even father children. (The wife may or may not be aware of her husband's cross-dressing.) Transvestites want to be left alone, and to cross-dress whenever they feel the urge.

Transsexuals, because they "feel they're in the wrong body," consider their sex organs a deformity. A male transsexual wants to live the life of a woman, and to engage in a heterosexual relationship (as a female) with a male. Because sex-change surgery is so drastic, doctors require that a candidate undergo a lengthy period of in-depth counseling and appropriate hormone therapy before surgery is performed. Hormone therapy causes breasts to develop, facial hair to soften and lessen, and the voice to rise in pitch. For the male, surgery involves removal of the penis and testicles, leaving enough skin to form an artificial vagina.

Questions Kids Ask

Can Every Couple Have a Baby?

Can every couple have a baby if they want to?

No, lots of husbands and wives want children with all their hearts, but they aren't able to physically produce a baby. Sometimes the wife's reproductive organs aren't quite right, maybe from birth. Sometimes the woman has a health problem, or she had an illness earlier that did permanent damage, so she can't become pregnant. Or the husband may have a problem, perhaps a low sperm count. That means either his semen contains fewer than the average number, of sperm or that the sperm are weak. (So when a husband and wife do have a baby, they thank God, as we did when you were born.)

When couples want children and are unable to conceive, it's called infertility, which is a major problem in our country. It's a good reminder to us to thank God for good health, and to take good care of the bodies He gives us.

Note to Parents: If you think your child is ready, you could use this question as a springboard to discuss how sexually transmitted diseases can silently damage an individual's reproductive system. See section on STDs.

Artificial Insemination

I heard that sometimes a woman can go to a doctor and have sperm put inside her to make a baby. What is that called?

Artificial insemination. Sperm is collected from the husband (or from a donor) and placed inside the wife's vagina with a medical instrument. If one of the sperm fertilizes her egg cell, pregnancy will result.

Note to Parents

Depending on how ready your child is, you may want to expand this simple, factual answer. Refer again to mutual love within marriage as the God-ordained basis for sexual intercourse and reproduction. That mutual love can be the reason for artificial insemination when the husband's sperm is used. However, mutual love is missing when sperm from a donor other than the husband is used.

What is a test-tube baby?

"Test-tube baby" is a slang term that isn't used much anymore for a child conceived through a complicated and costly procedure called in vitro fertilization (IVF). Couples who try IVF almost always have had lots of medical tests and treatment, but still don't have a baby. So IVF seems like the only way for such a wife and her husband to conceive a child. This process may need to be repeated several times, and doctors can't guarantee whether a woman will become pregnant at all. Here's how IVF works:

First, doctors inject the woman with hormones so her body will "ripen" several ova (eggs). Then they withdraw the ripe ova from the woman's ovaries. In a sterile laboratory procedure, they mix the ova with sperm from the woman's husband to fertilize the ova. When the tiny embryos begin to grow, the physician implants one or more directly into the woman's uterus. If all goes well, she'll have a normal pregnancy, and a healthy baby will be born nine months later.

There are moral ramifications involved in this procedure. Usually not all the embryos that are conceived are implanted in the woman's uterus. Some are either thrown away or frozen for later use. This creates a dilemma for Christians, who believe that life begins at conception and so should be treated with respect.

Adoption

Why don't people just adopt a baby if they can't give birth to one?

Many couples want to adopt a baby more than anything, but there aren't enough babies available and the cost to adopt those babies who are available to adopt is prohibitive to many people. One reason for this is that every year many pregnant women choose to have an abortion rather than to carry their baby to term. So those babies are never born, never available to be adopted. Another reason is that lots of unmarried mothers, even teenage moms, decide they want to raise their child alone, rather than to allow their babies to be adopted. So a childless couple may have to wait several years before they will have a chance to adopt. For some people, the wait is too long and they never get the opportunity to be parents.

People who are able to adopt a child love their child very, very much. After all, they wanted a child for so long before they got one. They feel just like other parents—they're proud of their child, they worry sometimes, and they scold sometimes. But mostly they just love their child and thank God for this gift they waited so long for.

Premature Babies

What does it mean when a baby is premature?

It means that the baby was born early—before the normal nine months. That almost always means there will be some problems. The lungs, for example, may not be fully developed for the baby to breathe properly. Hospitals are equipped to take care of such infants, and they have a lot of special equipment to help keep the baby alive until it can get along well on its own.

Miscarriage

What happens if a baby is born way too early—like at four or five months?

After the 16th week, this is called a miscarriage. Before that it's called a spontaneous abortion. Both happen unintentionally, and the reasons aren't always clear. The baby is seldom able to live on its own.

More Boys or Girls

Are there more boy babies or girl babies born?

There are about 105 males born for every 100 females. Doctors aren't quite sure why this is true.

What Determines Sex?

How does a baby get to be a boy or a girl, anyhow?

All cells contain chromosomes, which contain genes, which pass on traits you inherit, such as blue eyes or curly hair. There are 22 pairs of chromosomes that determine the inherited characteristics. But the 23rd pair of chromosomes is the one that decides what sex the child will be. Every female ovum contains an X chromosome. The ovum is fertilized by the male sperm, which may contain either an X chromosome or a Y chromosome. If the pair is XX, the child will be a girl; if XY, the child will be a boy.

Predicting Sex of Fetus

Can you tell whether a baby will be a boy or a girl before it's born?

Yes, but doctors usually order tests for other reasons. Sometimes the mother's age or the family history may increase the risk that the child will be born with problems. One test is called amniocentesis, in which the physician uses a syringe to withdraw a small amount of amniotic fluid that surrounds the fetus. The fluid is then studied in a laboratory. The tests will show whether the child will have certain inherited defects as well as the sex of the baby.

However, pregnant women routinely undergo sonograms (ultrasound) as a means of monitoring even healthy, normal pregnancies. This test employs high frequency sound waves beamed at the pregnant woman's abdomen. The waves bounce off the growing baby and the mother's organs, providing an image that's projected on a TV screen for evaluation. An experienced technician often can observe whether the fetus is male or female.

Most parents just pray that their baby will be healthy and normal. Besides, wondering what their baby will be is part of the fun!

Dangers to the Mother

Does the mother bleed a lot when she has a baby?

Usually not much at all—not enough to affect her normal blood count.

Do women ever die from having babies?

Occasionally a woman dies while giving birth. But if the mother has taken good care of herself, eaten the right foods, and seen her doctor regularly, the chances are good that she'll have a healthy delivery.

Delivery Position

Does a baby come out headfirst or feet first?

Babies are usually born headfirst. However, sometimes a baby comes out feet first or some other way. When it's time for the baby to be born, the doctor or midwife can tell whether the child is in the best position. He can also tell whether the mother is going to be able to deliver normally. (*Deliver* is the word that's used to mean "give birth.")

Most women have no problem. After all, God planned the whole process and made a female's uterus and vagina to stretch large enough for the baby to be born. But occasionally things don't work as well as they should.

If the doctor sees there will be a serious problem, he may decide to deliver the baby by a Caesarean or "C" section. Then the mother is taken into the surgical area of the hospital. A small cut is quickly made into her abdomen and then into her uterus. The baby is lifted out, and the uterus and abdomen are sewed shut. This operation doesn't take long, but it takes the mother a bit longer to get her strength back after the birth.

Twins and Multiple Births

What causes twins and triplets?

There are two types of twins—fraternal and identical. Some families have more than the usual number of twins, so it seems heredity plays a part. When a woman's ovary releases two or more ova or egg cells instead of the usual one, and they are fertilized, she will have more than one baby. If there are two egg cells, she will have fraternal twins. Each cell is entered by a separate sperm, so each has a separate placenta and is a completely different child. There may be one boy and one girl or the two may be of the same sex. Either way they're no more alike in looks than any other two kids in a family.

It's different for identical twins, however. When one ovum is fertilized by a single sperm, it may then split into two or more cells. If into two, it develops into two babies that share the same umbilical cord and placenta. Identical twins are always the same sex and usually look so much alike you can hardly tell them apart. They may even think alike!

Triplets and other multiple births may be either identical or fraternal. These days there seem to be more births of five or six or even more babies. One reason is that some women who have trouble becoming pregnant may consult a doctor who may give them what's known as a fertility drug. This is a substance that can cause a woman's body to release several egg cells. Unfortunately, in multiple births the babies are often born too early.

Birth Defects

Why are some babies born with birth defects?

The reasons are not completely known, but there are some clues. We know, for instance, that if the mother contracts German measles while she's pregnant, there's a higher likelihood that the baby will have birth defects or will not develop properly. Other diseases and viruses may also play a part. As medical science makes new discoveries, more and more problems are being overcome.

The best thing a pregnant woman can do is to get good medical care early; to eat good food and live sensibly; and to stay away from alcohol, tobacco, and medications (even over-the-counter drugs like aspirin). Sometimes, even though the mother does everything right, a child is born with problems. But the parents love the child because it's a part of them. And even though it makes them sad, they understand that God has a plan for their child, too.

The Teen Years:
Countdown to Lift-Off

Then our sons in their youth will be like well-nurtured plants, and our daughters will be like pillars carved to adorn a palace (Psalm 144:12).

Parents of older children are fond of saying to the parents of younger children: "Little children, little problems; big children, big problems."

The parents of younger children often resent this comment. Struggling to cope with rambunctious small ones, endlessly picking up after them, constantly watching out for them—these parents are understandably not convinced.

Yet in many ways this is true. Younger children do get into trouble that must be dealt with, of course. Their behavior may necessitate trips to the emergency room for broken bones, and they probably leave a trail of debris wherever they go. Yet most of these problems are relatively minor.

For the young person in high school and college, however, the potential for serious problems is much greater. Compared to having a pregnant teenage daughter, a child's broken bone is minor. Compared to one's child being responsible for an accident that caused someone's death, a broken window doesn't seem like much of a problem. Compared to a child being hooked on drugs—or dependent on alcohol—or living with someone outside of marriage, using foul language seems hardly worth mentioning.

This is not to say the latter behaviors are right or should be condoned; it's merely to point out that the problems one may face while raising a teenager can be vastly more complex. Thus the parent whose child has entered the teenage years often feels a kind of panic. "What can I do?" the parent asks.

By the time children reach this stage of life they are involved in many activities over which a parent has little control. One simply cannot go everywhere, oversee every activity, or select friends for one's teenager. Young people want to do things on their own—and rightly so. The child must become a responsible adult. Yet the perils we parents see are very real, and our fears are understandable. What to do?

There is one essential above all others: Pray. That may sound hopelessly simplistic or like a stick-your-head-in-the-sand kind of answer, but in truth it's the only answer that carries any assurance. As Christians we can confidently turn our children over to the care and guidance of our gracious heavenly Father.

And what better answer do we have? We are limited; God is limitless. We see only what our eyes comprehend; God sees everywhere. As that familiar Bible verse puts it:

> *For He will command His angels concerning you to guard*
> *you in all your ways; they will lift you up in their hands, so*
> *that you will not strike your foot against a stone*
> *(Psalm 91:11–12).*

That verse is true for our children, too!

Surprise! Parents Are Still Role Models

As always, our children are watching us, absorbing our values, our behavior. This is true even though they may ridicule our style of dress, the way we comb our hair, the car we drive, our lifestyle, even the language we use. Most children would never dream of admitting it, and probably don't realize it's true, yet we parents, by the way we live, are a major influence on their lives—now and in the future. Sooner or later most young adults begin to espouse largely the same values as their parents.

Remember Lauren, who spent most of her 13th and 14th years in her room? "The whole thing was crazy," said her mother, "but she eventually came around. By the time she was about 15½ she began to mellow. She would actually sit around the family room with the rest of us now and then. By 16 she was almost getting pleasant, and by 17 we were all on good terms again. At 18 she was telling her younger brother and sister to pay attention to us—that they didn't know how lucky they were to have us for parents. Kids! Who can figure them out?"

Teenagers also get their concept of what marriage is from us. When they see that our marriage relationship is deep and mutually enriching, when they sense husband and wife meet each other's needs, they see a clear witness that even in this world of distorted values a couple can have a satisfying marriage.

"My mom and dad were divorced when I was a small child," said Paul, "and I spent a lot of time with my best friend, Tim. I loved going to his house. That's where I first began to see what marriage could be. Tim's mom and dad were still in love—even after all those years and three kids. I couldn't believe it when we'd walk into the kitchen and they'd be hugging and kissing.

"One time I got up the nerve to ask Tim's dad why their marriage had worked, and we both had a long talk. He said one thing that stood out in my mind: 'We both try to put Christ first. And we try to love each other—accept each other—as Christ would. We fail, of course, all the time. But we keep on trying—and, especially, we keep on depending on the forgiveness we have because of Jesus. I guess if we have a secret, that's it.'

"I never forgot that conversation," said Paul. "I suppose Denise and I might have broken up long ago if I hadn't had Tim's folks to remember. They proved to me that it's possible to stay married—and stay in love."

Because of our influence on young people, it's apparent that keeping our own marriage healthy is still our number one priority. For where else would we want them to get their values concerning what it means to be married? From the movies? From television? From books? Most of us would answer with an emphatic "No!" Yet those are the major sources of information and influence for young people.

Young People Want to Know

Young people are curious, especially about sex. Here are questions written down and turned in by high school freshmen during a youth Bible class:

- How do you know if sex is right for you?
- How do you know if your partner cares or if you are just being used?
- How often do couples have intercourse?
- Can sperm swim through your jeans?
- How do you stop if you really feel you love your partner and would like to have sex, but are afraid of getting pregnant?
- What are advantages and disadvantages of different types of birth control?

- What are the long-term effects of the birth-control pill?
- Is it true you can't get pregnant if the boy pulls out in time?
- If sex is safe with a condom, what's the big deal?
- At what time of the month is a girl most likely to get pregnant? Is any time safe?
- Is it safe if a pregnant girl has sex?

Surprised? These are the questions on the minds of young teenagers. Christian teenagers. And they may be the subjects most parents would rather not discuss with their children.

"I feel uncomfortable talking about sex with our kids," said Latrice thoughtfully. "They're too young to have sex anyway. If we teach them everything, would they think we're giving them permission to have intercourse? And if they are going all the way, I don't want to know about it! I don't think I could handle it. Besides, they've had sex education classes at school and they know all the facts—probably more than I do."

Many parents feel like Latrice. Yet when we don't talk with our teens, we're out of the picture altogether. We have no chance to share our own Christian values—God's formula for living responsibly.

Knowledgeable Young People?

The truth is that although today's young people seem sophisticated, many have faulty ideas regarding sex. Much of their information—and misinformation—comes from the media.

Consider this: Between the ages of 12 and 17, teenagers watch an average of 22 hours of TV per week—or about three hours per day. So one researcher's findings shouldn't surprise us: Typical graduating high school seniors will have watched 22,000 hours of television, twice as many hours as they've spent in the classroom.

Now estimate how often daytime and prime time programming suggests or depicts sexual behavior, usually between people who are not married to each other. (Try keeping score for a week!) One high school freshman was quoted as saying, "A lot of what I've learned about sex, I've learned from the soaps. ... The people just fall into each other's arms and it's beautiful. That's how I'd like sex to be for me." So why should we be surprised that recent surveys show the majority of people ages 13 to 18 see nothing wrong with premarital intercourse?

The Chilling Statistics

Those attitudes are reflected in the rising rates of sexually transmitted disease (STD). Ponder these facts:

- STDs infect three million teenagers annually.

- 1.3 million new cases of gonorrhea occur annually; strains of gonorrhea have developed that are resistant to penicillin.

- It's estimated that every year from 60,000 to 100,000 young
American women are made sterile by the HIV virus, gonorrhea,
or chlamydia: most are unaware that they have the disease.
(Statistics for other countries are similarly alarming.)

- The infection rate for chlamydia is highest among girls 15 to 19.

- As many as a third of sexually active teenagers have genital warts.

- The AIDS rate among teenagers is climbing, and because of the
long incubation period, almost certainly many teens are infected
and unaware.

But there's additional evidence that times are changing—and not
for the better:

- Most sexual intercourse between teenage boys and girls takes
place in the home of one or the other while the parents are away.

- Each year more than one million teenage girls in the U.S. become
pregnant—one in nine women ages 15 to 19 and one in five who
are sexually active.

- Each year more than 500,000 U.S. teenage females will carry their
babies to term. More than 400,000 young women under the age of
20 will have an abortion. Approximately 14 percent of teenage
pregnancies will end in miscarriage.

- Within a year, almost one in five will become pregnant again.
More than 31 percent will become pregnant a second time within
two years.

- More than 90 of every 100 unwed U.S. teen mothers choose to
parent their infants, usually with little social stigma attached.

Christian young people are different, but perhaps not as much as
we wish. A survey conducted well into the '90s queried more than
1,200 teens attending a national youth gathering of their mainline
conservative Christian denomination. Of these young, active church
members, 47 percent viewed premarital sexual relationships as "always
wrong." Nearly 32 percent okayed premarital sex when two people
love each other, while over 17 percent were unsure. (Similar studies
among other church youth yield much the same results.)

Actions do speak louder than words, however. Another source recently surveyed Christian teens and came up with these findings among "church youth who admit to having sexual intercourse":

Age 12	Age 13	Age 14	Age 15	Age 16	Age 17
4%	10%	20%	29%	46%	57%

These statistics are not meant to frighten—only to point out how necessary it is that we help our children develop strong Christian moral values. If we regard these numbers as "statistics," we miss the point. The numbers represent living, breathing teenagers; friends and fellow students of our own daughters and sons.

Scare Tactics Are Not the Answer

Statistics are not likely to impress our children. Feeling immortal, as teenagers often do, they seem unimpressed by the danger of AIDS. Pregnancy? Young people, especially girls, still cling to the idea that "It couldn't happen to me." Despite stepped-up sex education in the schools, despite the advertising barrage, despite freely available birth control products, most teens pass them up. Some may be uninformed. More often they envision being swept away on a romantic wave of passion—and condoms and other birth control options mar that image.

In fact, today's teenagers often plan precisely when they'll "do it," regarding their first instance of sexual intercourse as a sort of marker of maturity. Counselors report that among teens, pregnancy frequently is no accident.

Listen to Andrea, a mother at age 16: "I guess I really wanted to get pregnant. I wanted to show everyone—especially my parents— that I was grown-up and they couldn't tell me what to do. You know? They don't care about me anyhow. No one does. But a baby of my own ... well, my baby would always love me, I thought, no matter what. And no one could ever take it away from me. Besides, school was boring!

"So I had my baby, a little girl. My parents had kicked me out, so I went on welfare and it's been rough. Sometimes when I've been up half the night with Sarah and I'm dead on my feet, I think I must have been crazy to get into this mess. If school was a pain, having a kid is 100 times worse! ... And the father? Oh, you mean Jay. When he heard I was pregnant and wouldn't get an abortion, he left. He didn't love me—nobody does! But I have a new boyfriend now. ... He says he really cares ..."

Unfortunately, Andrea will probably be pregnant again before very long—and alone—and searching for "love." We live in a world where such actions are not only tolerated but expected—where young people are often under considerable pressure to "do it."

Strength for Living in Today's Society

Christian young people also live in this world. They feel the same emotions, struggle with the same temptations as their peers. Although we may wish it were so, our children don't go through life encased in a protective bubble. But we parents can help them learn to be strong. How? By being open and accepting in our conversations with them. By talking of how Christ's teachings relate to our lives with others. Share these words of Jesus with your teen:

> "Love the Lord your God with all your heart and with all
> your soul and with all your mind." This is the first and
> greatest commandment. And the second is like it: "Love your
> neighbor as yourself" (Matthew 22:37–39).

These are the fundamentals Christ would have us remember in any kind of relationship. Sexual permissiveness, with its great potential for causing emotional and physical harm, contradicts these principles. Using people, achieving our own emotional gratification at the expense of another, hurting another human being, are all things we would not want done to us, all evidence of selfishness. And selfishness is now—as it always was—sin.

Christ knew, of course, that the rest of the world would behave differently and attempt to influence us. The Bible has the key to dealing with that pressure, too.

> Do not conform any longer to the pattern of this world,
> but be transformed by the renewing of your mind
> (Romans 12:2).

To live as Christ's people, to be strong enough to be different, does not come from our own efforts. Rather we allow God to make us strong—from the inside out!

It's Never Easy

Even so, living the Christian life is never easy. Changing attitudes make it much more difficult, especially for teens. "I'd hate to be young these days," said Juana, frowning. "It's got to be much harder. Lots of us toed the mark only because we were scared silly. The neighbors were always peeking out their windows, and the older people in our town and our church kept an eye on us. And we knew it! Aunts, uncles, and cousins all made it their business to lecture us if they thought we had it coming. As for contraception, such products were hard to get— if we'd even known what to do with them. And if a girl got pregnant, well, her whole family was disgraced.

"Now families are scattered, and I'm not sure they'd speak up, anyhow. In fact, I don't know if I would. … I guess we all have the attitude that 'It's not my problem.' Today a teenager can easily buy birth control products—probably from a clerk who doesn't even look surprised. And unwed teenage mothers are bringing their babies to school with them. Seems to me a teenager nowadays has to be good just because he or she wants to—because they sure don't get much help!"

Juana is right. But in spite of today's permissiveness, there is still a large segment of teens who do not choose to engage in sexual activity. For example, take the example cited earlier—those 1,200 conservative Christian teens attending a youth gathering. Asked about their own sexual activity, 77 percent of the girls and over 68 percent of the boys responded, "Never engaged in intercourse." More than nine percent had intercourse previously, but currently abstained, while another nine percent regularly engaged in sexual intercourse. Yes, our teens may express opinions and attitudes that shock us, and we're foolish to think they're not tempted. But if we automatically assume they're sexually active, who could blame them for feeling, "What's the use? I'm pronounced guilty no matter what I do!" Resentment and alienation result.

Those Inevitable Conflicts

Sometimes, in spite of our best efforts, a situation arises where our children feel we don't trust them. We may refuse permission to go on a weekend trip with a group of new friends, for instance.

"The way we handle such things," says Jane, "is to tell our daughter, 'Look, we trust you as a person. But we don't feel you have the maturity and experience yet to make all of your own decisions. You could end up in a situation you're not equipped to handle. So we have to say no.' Our daughter seems able to accept that explanation without too much hassle because it doesn't attack her personally."

As parents, we have a right to say, "Our family rule is … " Teenagers want to know the acceptable limits, even when they protest.

In fact it's often a relief when they can say, "My parents want me in by midnight."

Should our children occasionally come home later than the agreed-upon time, we'll accept their reasonable excuse. After all, young people do have car trouble at times. They do go to concerts and movies that run later than they expect. They do become deeply engrossed in talking with a friend and lose track of time. (Haven't we done the same at times with our own good friends?)

When we know our young people to be generally reliable, we can show our trust, even when circumstances seem contrary. If we believe the subject demands discussion, a good way to begin is by saying, "Perhaps you think I won't understand, but I promise I'll try. Could we talk about it?"

It is, of course, a different situation if we've had problems with our child lying to us. In general, we'll do well to "put the best construction on everything." For if we show that we believe our children and emphasize the importance of being trustworthy, more often than not they'll try to live up to our expectations.

The Best Kind of Parental Love

As Christian parents, we'll avoid needless confrontations except when our teens are acting in a manner clearly contrary to God's will. "My parents were really great, all those years when I was a teenager and giving them a hard time," says Erica. "Deep down I knew they loved me, no matter what, and that they were proud of me as a person, even when they didn't like what I had done. Sure, I disappointed them sometimes—and they me—but we were a family and our love went on. I can't tell you what that meant to me when everything else in my life often seemed upside down."

Our teens need our respect, as well, if they're going to respect themselves and others. For instance, we'd never say to one of our own friends (especially in front of contemporaries), "Angelo, are you ever going to get your hair cut? Must you always look so shaggy?" Nor would we appreciate it if we were at a gathering with friends and someone said to us, "Are you sure you want to have dessert? You can barely get your pants buttoned as it is!" Neither would we call to an adult departing with a date, "Now remember what I told you. Act like a lady and behave yourself!"

Yet some parents are prone to issue similar reminders in ringing tones, regardless of how many people are present. Such insensitivity can immeasurably damage a child's self-esteem.

All this may seem far removed from sexuality. But when we respect our young people, their own feelings of self-worth are strengthened. And a healthy self-image is necessary to develop into an adult able to relate on all levels, including sex.

Communication Is Important

The attitude we want to cultivate with our young people is that they can tell us anything at any time. However, we should be ready to really listen. "I remember trying to talk to my dad," says Jordan. "But he never heard what I said. I could sense he was just waiting for me to pause so he could jump in and tell me what I was doing wrong. He always had the 'perfect solution' all ready to lay out for me.

"What *I* thought, what *I* felt, didn't really matter. He didn't care. He was more concerned with giving answers than with hearing questions. After a while I just avoided talking with him because we had no real communication."

Jordan makes a good point. Communication consists of two parts—talking *and* listening. "I never really knew how to listen until I read a book on effective communication," said Jennifer. "Now I try to follow those guidelines. I listen to the kids and then repeat what I think they've said before answering. They do the same. At first it seemed awkward to all of us, but now it's a habit. It's great! At last we really hear each other."

Another part of true communication is hearing what's behind the words. When we talk with our teenagers, for instance, we'll want to know what they're feeling, not just surface details. For we can only reach understanding when we perceive what's inside.

Open communication doesn't require that our young people tell us every last detail of every thought, word, and deed. For example, most of the time teenagers won't get too explicit about the details of their dates, nor should we attempt to pry. But once they've confided in us, if we then use that information to scold or threaten or make cutting remarks, they'll not share secret thoughts with us again. And who can blame them?

When we talk with our child about sexuality, we'll want to verbalize and communicate our feelings as well. If we're uncomfortable, maybe we're reflecting our own parents' attitudes with us. Those old patterns die hard. Even parents who feel very emancipated may find themselves hesitant about discussing sex with an aware teenager. It's okay to feel self-conscious and uneasy. Trust the reassurance of professionals: Our awkwardness is unimportant. What counts is that we open up communication, that we listen as well as talk, and that our child feels respected rather than put down.

Be Sure to Speak the Same Language

Over recent years terminology has changed. Adults use words that don't necessarily mean the same thing to adolescents. So we may not be communicating as clearly as we suppose, even when we congratulate ourselves on our "open and frank" conversations. For example:

- Many teens today consider the word *virgin* to mean an individual who has "only" engaged in oral or anal sex.
- Both oral or anal sex typically are believed to protect against contracting (or transmitting) most sexually transmitted diseases (STDs).
- Oral sex is considered the foolproof means of birth control and has gained widespread acceptance by teens.
- It's not unusual for Christian young people to maintain that admonitions against "premarital sex" apply only to actual sexual intercourse. So long as the male's penis does not penetrate the female's vagina, anything else is okay.

Despite more education about the transmission of STDs, misinformation abounds. We need to be sure teenagers understand the facts. (More detailed information is provided in the question-and-answer section at the end of this chapter, under the heading "Talking to Teens about Responsible Sexuality.")

For instance, young people *must* be aware that even if condoms are used, even if sex play stops short of penetration, syphilis, genital herpes, and other STDs can be transmitted via bodily secretions. This can be from genital/genital contact, from oral/genital contact, or from either oral sex or anal sex. In fact, even skin-to-skin contact can spread human papilloma virus (HPV), now recognized as the major causative agent for cervical and penile cancer.

Although we may look at our children and think, "This is beyond them!" it's vital to bear in mind that today's young people are more sexualized than ever before. We can blame the influence of television and movies or changing morals or whatever we prefer. But the truth is that more young people engage in early sexual activity than they did a generation ago. And the dangers to their well-being have escalated markedly.

Changing Patterns

In the past it was assumed that every young male wanted to progress from kissing to touching to intercourse. Girls were considered more inhibited and likely to be coerced into sexual activity by their boyfriends. Today many teenage girls are quite aggressive and may openly approach a young man.

"I took Meghan to a movie the other night and, boy, did she come on to me," says Andrew. "She kept leaning against me in the theater, and after the show she told me her parents were gone for the weekend, so why didn't we go to her place and have sex? She said she's on the pill, so why worry?

"I didn't know what to do—I hardly knew her! So I told her I had to get the car home so my sister could go to work, and I left in a hurry. Most of the guys I knew would give their right arm to be with Meghan. Is there something wrong with me?"

Young people of both sexes need reassurance that they're not "undersexed" or abnormal in any way when they choose not to become sexually active. Rather, they are to be commended for their wisdom and maturity, for sticking to their own values in spite of pressure.

Today both the young male and the young female may see intercourse as a conquest, proof that they're worldly wise and attractive. Both may matter-of-factly expect to get or give sexual favors in reward for a big date. After all, they've seen it on television and in the movies: date, come home, and end up in bed. It's a standard procedure!

So each has a responsibility for setting the tone for the relationship in the beginning, quietly and kindly. Even so, the old arguments will likely be used:

- "But I can't stand it! Do you want me to go crazy or something?"
- "It's just not natural to deny ourselves when we both care about each other."
- "Of course I don't just want your body! I care about you as a person."
- "How can we have a meaningful relationship without sex?"
- "Sure, I'll always respect you, no matter what."
- Etc., etc., etc.

The logic is as faulty as it ever was. With the added pressure of today's permissive society, young people need to think carefully through their own values—form their own solid foundation. It's helpful, too, when youngsters understand not only their own bodies but those of the other sex.

Abstinence Education Is Not Enough!

Today many people, especially Christians, believe that young people simply need abstinence education. Just replace the typical school sex education classes with a curriculum to teach teenagers to say no, and all will be well, they say.

Certainly educating teens on the pitfalls of premarital sex is helpful. Yet counselors observe it's not enough simply to tell young people with raging hormones to "just say no." We also need to provide *reasons* for avoiding sex. We live in a free-and-easy society. Children grow up learning that they can do anything, be anything, have anything. So why should we expect adolescents to readily deny themselves what their bodies crave? After all, many of their peers indulge in sexual relationships and receive little or no criticism—from fellow students or from adults. Many adults echo this sentiment: "Well, you can't fight their hormones. I just hope they're using protection!"

People of any age willingly sacrifice comfort and satisfaction for the sake of a larger goal. Our task is to provide a goal—a *purpose*—so attractive that our teens set aside their present desires for the sake of a magnificent future reward. What's called for is a *vision* to live up to. When we talk with our young people we need to keep a balance of prohibitions and promises.

The "Manufacturer's Handbook"

Consider how we present the Ten Commandments to our children. Do we tick off "Thou shalt nots" as if these were the "Ten Prohibitions"? Or do we point out that the Ten Commandments are part of the Handbook issued by the Manufacturer, who wants His product (human beings) to function most effectively?

In the Sixth Commandment, for instance, God says, "You shall not commit adultery." There is more to this commandment than just a physical prohibition. Out of love and respect for God, we want to honor the body He gave us by living a sexually pure and decent life in all that we say and do as outlined in 1 Corinthians 6:18–20:

> *Flee from sexual immorality. All other sins a man commits are outside his body, but he who sins sexually sins against his own body. Do you not know that your body is a temple of the Holy Spirit, who is in you, whom you have received from*

God? You are not your own; you were bought at a price.
Therefore honor God with your body.

Also in this commandment, God is asking us to honor marriage. God modeled marriage after Christ's relationship with the church, as St. Paul so eloquently described:

Husbands, love your wives, just as Christ loved the church
and gave Himself up for her to make her holy, cleansing her
by the washing with water through the word, and to present
her to Himself as a radiant church, without stain or wrinkle
or any other blemish, but holy and blameless
(Ephesians 5:25–27).

We can't ever forget that our offspring are at the age when sexual interest is heightened and brand-new emotions threaten to overwhelm. So we need to set these words in a context appropriate for the young individual. To "lead a sexually pure and decent life" plainly applies to both sexes, all ages, all situations of life. That's a given.

A natural bridge is to discuss how this commandment ties in with what they've been told in school classes. Beginning in the primary grades, youngsters learn about AIDS and sexually transmitted diseases (STDs). We could ask our teenagers (who usually consider themselves invulnerable) what material they've covered.

Were they taught that medical researchers declare that when two people engage in sex, each also is having sex with *every other person* with whom the partner *ever* had sexual relations? Are they aware that obvious signs of infection may be absent? The dormancy period for HIV infection has been proven to last beyond 10 years. Some STDs, such as genital herpes, can be spread by sexual contact that stops short of actual intercourse—even by oral contact. So only sexual purity guarantees no possibility of contracting (or transmitting) a sexually transmitted disease and ensures no risk of pregnancy.

"Love" Is More Than a Feeling

Our Creator also addresses sexual behavior within marriage. Society emphasizes "love" (the emotion) as the total answer to happiness, before and after marriage. Yet these words to husbands and wives tell how to *do* love. Long-time married couples know that "honor," i.e., mutual respect, is crucial if love is to endure. When one marriage partner breaks the marriage covenant, other "dominoes" will topple, one by one. Trust will erode. The husband and wife's relationship will be weakened. Even with forgiveness and counseling, their marriage may be irreparably damaged or not survive. A couple may remain in their marriage yet wage their personal version of The Cold War within their home. Children may feel torn between their parents.

It's not stretching credibility to say that casual sex, even a single encounter, could place at risk one's life—or one's ability to have children. So when God gives us the Sixth Commandment, is He being punitive or protective? Did He set out to "spoil our fun" or to show us how to maintain a fulfilling life? Is He handing us a set of rules just to watch us squirm? Or is He revealing how His beloved children can escape many of the common difficulties we observe in the personal lives of so many around us?

Prohibitions or promises, negative or positive—it's our call, in this as in every other discussion we have with our children.

Why Do We Hold Our Personal Values?

Before we discuss values with our young people, we must do some personal soul-searching. What do we believe? Why? Have we thought it through in light of today or are we just parroting words and slogans? If it's the latter, be assured our youngster will see right through it and discount what we say. Especially if we begin, "When I was your age, young people wouldn't dream of ..."

But talk we must. There are many subjects to discuss, and it helps to remember these facts:

• Casual sex can never be what God intended the sexual relationship to be. People who consider sex as a fleeting encounter or "just fun" usually have never known anything deeper.

• There's no medical or psychological evidence that postponing sexual intercourse causes any lasting physical or emotional harm to males or females.

• The dangers of AIDS and other sexually transmitted diseases are very real. Because many STDs exhibit no outward symptoms, an infected person may be unaware, but contagious, nevertheless. The AIDS virus can incubate for more than 10 years before the infected individual tests positive, yet that person can transmit the virus all along.

• When two people have intercourse, each also is, in a sense, having sex with every other sexual partner in the other's life. So the more sexual contact one has, the higher the risk of contacting an STD.

- There is no absolutely safe period when a female can be assured of not becoming pregnant.
- Other than abstinence, there is no 100 percent foolproof method of birth control, even when directions are followed correctly. Even when the male withdraws his penis before ejaculation, there may be early leakage of sperm before withdrawal. Pregnancy can result, and diseases can be transmitted.
- Teenage mothers and their babies are much more likely to experience health complications. The younger the mother, the greater the hazard.
- Babies born to teenage mothers are two to three times as likely to die during the first year. Lifelong, such children more often display lower intellectual and academic achievement, plus problems of self-control and social behavior.
- Teenage mothers often spend their lives on welfare. A large portion of the federal budget for the Temporary Assistance for Needy Families program goes to households where the mother gave birth in her teens.
- Women who become mothers in their teen years are likely to have jobs with less status, lower incomes, and less satisfaction all through their lives.
- People who become parents during their teens may be more likely to become child abusers, perhaps because of resentment over what they've missed.
- 80 percent of teenage marriages end in divorce within five years.

Be sure that both you and your teenager speak the same language. Many teens today, according to counselors, consider "virgin" to mean an individual who has "only" engaged in oral or anal sex. Others view this practice as a means of birth control. Both practices are very dangerous, and both expose them to sexually transmitted diseases, including AIDS.

Better Too Soon Than Too Late

It's important to talk with our children early, before they close up like a clam. By the time young people are dating (or their friends are), their perspective will have changed, their opinions formed. Then our effort to communicate Christian values may seem like a contrary, personal judgment of them or their peers.

We start by being frank, by communicating our love and acceptance. Perhaps we might begin by saying: "I'll answer any questions you want to throw at me. If I don't know the answers, I'll find them. I'll listen to your opinions and try to understand what you believe and why. I hope you'll do the same for me.

"Sometimes young people think they 'owe' each other sex. Some may think having intercourse will prove they're liberated. But liberation means being free, not giving in to someone else's standards. Neither your best friend nor the crowd nor the person you date—nor society—should dictate what you do. And because you're a Christian that's especially true."

"Love" Isn't Always Love

"You see, many times what seems like 'love' is simply sexual attraction—something you could feel with many different people at various periods of your life. But to love someone—to enter into a sexual relationship (and as Christians we believe that must be as a married couple)—involves much more: commitment for life, faithfulness, respecting the other's right to be an individual, willingness to put the other person before oneself, the desire to build a life together. It means 'we' is more important than 'I.'

"And contrary to what most people think, love is not just an emotion; it's a daily decision. Most people aren't ready for that until they've had time to find out who they are themselves and what they want to do with their lives—until they've developed the ability to see themselves and each other clearly and logically, accepting each other as they are.

"It also means being ready to take total responsibility for one's own life and actions, as well as the responsibility of a child, because that's always a possibility. It means being ready to put aside one's own goals, if necessary, for the good of the family.

"If you enter into a sexual relationship outside of marriage, you may be letting yourself in for a lot of pain—and cause pain for others, too. Part of that pain is sneaking around. Think about God's plan for us: a husband and wife committed to life together, secure in each other's love, with time to grow together and work out any problems. God's plan works so well, in fact, that anything else is second best."

This can also be a good time to discuss again some of the material from the previous chapter, which deals with the sexual relationship in more detail. Of course, we won't deliver all this information nonstop. Nor can we now sit back and say, "Well, that takes care of that!" Our young people are constantly changing and will have new concerns and questions at various times along the way to maturity. That's why communication is best when it's easy and open—and ongoing.

Backing Up Words with Action

Young people demonstrate growing maturity by their behavior and by adopting a sound set of values. We parents play a major part in establishing those values. All through the growing-up years we try to live by the principles we proclaim. Now that's even more vital, for nothing more easily makes a young person cynical about adult integrity than a do-as-I-say-not-as-I-do attitude.

"My dad's always lecturing me about honesty," said 17-year-old Jason, "and I used to be proud of him because I thought he was different. Lately I've been finding out he's not. Like when he was bragging about what he got away with on his income tax return. Or when the restaurant cashier gave him change for a 20-dollar bill and he'd only given her a 10. Next time he gives me that old honesty speech, I'm gonna tell him what I really think!"

Parents give other kinds of conflicting messages, too. For instance, we may say that we want our youngsters to avoid emotional entanglements. Yet we may actually push them into early dating and/or sexual activity (usually without realizing it). As an example, our daughter may not be as popular as we'd like, so we pressure her to date—anyone. Or we may be vaguely fearful a child could have homosexual tendencies and view dating as proof to the contrary. Sometimes we get personal satisfaction from knowing our youngster is much sought after.

If we want our young people to heed our counsel, they need assurance that we live what we say.

Unflattering Comparisons

Today's youngsters appear to be brighter, more talented and attractive, more in control. Indeed, parents may even feel uncomfortable around their teenagers. Father may become newly conscious that his largest measurement is now around his stomach instead of his chest. He stands next to his handsome son, who towers above him, and is acutely conscious of thinning hair and sagging jowls.

For her part, Mother sees a daughter in a bikini or short shorts, notes the fresh, unwrinkled face and sparkling eyes, and sighs. Did she ever look that beautiful? Suddenly both parents feel old and dumpy, a bit self-conscious around their own children and their friends.

But it's quite possible for parents to be friends with their children, without in any way being in competition. It means that we esteem ourselves as we are—and our children as individuals in their own right. It's important frequently to reaffirm our love, too. An arm around the shoulders, a pat on the back—just simple human contact— is all it takes. The youngster may react by seeming uncomfortable or impatient, but that simply reflects the process of growing away from the parent-child relationship.

Our acceptance and affection, the way we relate to our young people now, will have a lasting effect. The satisfying true friendships we desire with our grown children have their roots in these teen years.

Handling the Unthinkable

Suppose, however, that we've tried to do everything right, but it all seems to go wrong. Suppose that our child makes foolish choices, perhaps with devastating, permanent fallout. What approach should we take?

We should model the same reaction that our gracious God has when we sin: love that seeks first of all to lead to repentance. We indeed identify the sin as sin. We don't excuse or whitewash it. But the goal of our speaking God's Law to our child is to lead him or her to repentance and renewed faith in Jesus. Love gives us no alternative. For if we take a you-made-your-bed-now-lie-in-it attitude, what will we accomplish? This young person needs our emotional support and our tender acceptance, even though we in no way approve what has happened.

For we, too, have made—and will make—mistakes. It is sin, yes, but Jesus Christ died to redeem us from sin. All sin. Can we do less than to stand by our children through such a time and try to help them find direction? True, there is pain for everyone involved. But we—and our young people—may well grow through pain.

Our child inevitably will do some honest self-appraisal. Our pride in our own strength will dissipate. Our heart(s) will be more teachable. That's when the Holy Spirit can use our anguish to strengthen us and make us more like Jesus. When we feel discouraged, let's read Romans 3:21–27 and 5:1–11. Then lay down our load of blame and despair at the foot of the cross. That's what God's grace is all about.

The Key to Surviving Parenthood

As Christians, struggling to be understanding, patient parents of teenagers, we'll display trust in our children; work to strengthen our relationship; frequently reinforce their self-esteem and sense of identity; talk openly—and listen. We'll daily commit our young people to God's loving care and ask His forgiveness for their mistakes and our own. And we'll take courage from the words of 1 Peter 4:8:

> *Above all, love each other deeply, because love covers over a multitude of sins.*

Questions Parents Ask

Dating Age

What's the right age for dating?

There is no "right" age. It depends on an individual family's standards and the maturity of the young people involved. Often counselors advise dating a variety of people. There's another wise perspective, however. *Very few individuals marry without first dating the person with whom they fall in love!* Those who are wise date only individuals who possess the values they'd be comfortable living with for the rest of their life.

Together with your teenager, why not draw up a list of desirable qualities he or she wants in a marriage partner. (Don't overlook faith in Christ.) Wouldn't individuals who display those characteristics also prove to be good choices for dating? Remember, too, that many long-term happily married couples never dated anyone else.

Friendships

Can teenage males and females really "just be friends"?

Today's teens seem able to have real friendships with those of the other sex without any romantic entanglement. Perhaps they've learned to consider people as individuals, and look for qualities that would make for good friends, disregarding gender.

Teens Entertaining when Parents Are Gone

My husband travels a lot in his work, and he often asks me to go along. I enjoy it, and our children are teenagers now, able to care for themselves. But I don't feel right leaving them alone. I'm afraid they'll give a wild party or something. Am I being silly?

Many parents as a general principle forbid their children to entertain anyone in the home when they're not present. Since researchers now tell us that most sexual activity between teenagers occurs in the home while the parents are gone, it seems prudent to avoid providing opportunities for temptation. (One alternative would be to limit guests to a specified number of the same sex as your child.)

One way to approach this subject without insulting the teenager's sense of trustworthiness and maturity is to say something like this: "Of course we trust you. We trust your integrity and your values and your good intentions. But we don't think you've had enough experience just yet for us to trust your judgment. We feel the same way about your friends. That's the reason for our family policy that you don't have anyone in the house when we're not here.

"You probably don't agree, but we love you and care about what could happen to you more than anything, so this is the way our family will operate."

This policy could be reviewed as your teenagers grow older and show more maturity. But even then you'll probably want to lay down some conditions. You may also wish to emphasize that you don't want your youngsters going to a friend's home when his or her parents aren't around. However, this is much more difficult to enforce.

Foul Language

My teenager has a foul mouth. When I scold, his reply is, "Don't be so old-fashioned! All my friends talk this way." Is that true?

Children and teenagers often feel they automatically become more grown-up if they use such language. Or they may simply be reflecting the language they hear at school; perhaps some of their friends talk this way. On the other hand, some children delight in using such language and/or in telling dirty jokes precisely because they know they'll get a shocked reaction from adults.

As Christians, of course, we're to be different from the world, and the Bible gives us many guidelines:

> *Keep your tongue from evil and your lips from speaking lies (Psalm 34:13).*

> *Set a guard over my mouth, O LORD; keep watch over the door of my lips (Psalm 141:3).*

Rather than shame our child or try to manipulate behavior through conveying guilt, we Christian parents can quietly state: "This is what the Bible teaches, and this is our standard as a Christian family. Therefore, please don't use that kind of language in our home." You can't control what your child says when away from you, of course, but you have a right to establish firm principles within your home.

In addition, you can point out that many people are offended by such language. And since people are often judged by the way they talk, your child may miss out on some friendships or opportunities if speech standards are low.

If your child seems to have a need to use obscenities constantly, try to find time for a long talk. Are there deep problems that trouble him? Is the youngster feeling isolated or rejected, either from his peers or his family? Does this young person have a low self-image, a continual need to prove unworthiness by flouting society and family standards?

If, after such a discussion, your youngster still seems to have a compulsion to use foul language, it may be the sign of deeply rooted problems and you may wish to seek professional counseling.

Pornography

I found some "dirty" pictures in my son's room. How should I have handled it?

At some time in their growing-up years, most boys possess some pornographic and/or erotic materials, which are increasingly easy to obtain. Often youngsters think this gives them a pictorial illustration of "what it's all about." After all, they reason, how else will they know what to do when their time comes? There are women's magazines with male centerfolds, and there is pornography produced for females, so young girls may also acquire such material.

The human body is not "dirty." Some of the greatest, most enduring works of art portray the nude human form. Christians see the human body as a marvel of God's creation—which it is! Pornography, however, is meant to be shocking, meant to be lewd. Pornography is a distortion of what God intends for the body.

Should you discover pornographic material belonging to your child, resist the impulse to launch into a lecture. Your loud, intense pronouncements will only make this forbidden fruit sweeter. Rather, recognize that sexual curiosity is natural.

But you may want to have a low-key discussion. Look at the pornography together. Pornography almost always portrays human beings in a dehumanizing manner. Typically a female is shown as an object, being used by a male for his own sexual gratification. Or the poses are deliberately intended to arouse the viewer sexually. In other words, pornography reduces sexuality to a function and the human body to a thing; it also does away completely with the idea of a caring and committed relationship between man and woman. This destroys

God's concept of personhood. And we all want to be appreciated for the person we are, not just as gratification machines.

The greatest danger of heavy pornography viewing is that these attitudes may be absorbed by impressionable young people. They may not yet have the insight to realize that a sexual relationship involves more—much more—than two sets of sex organs. In most cases, an open, frank discussion with an understanding parent will tarnish the glitter of such material. Most young people are extremely idealistic. Once they recognize the dehumanizing character of such trash, it will likely lose most of its appeal.

Explaining Sexual Intercourse to Teens

I told my youngsters about the "facts of life" long ago. Can't I assume they understand all about sexual intercourse?

No, because they are older now and will comprehend differently. They're also more personally interested in the subject. You may wish to say something like this:

"God gave males and females a very special marriage gift called sexual intercourse. Husbands and wives love each other very much—so much that there are times when they want to be close and caress each other and touch each other. They want to know how much they love and care for each other, and words just don't seem to be enough.

"When the husband thinks how much he loves his wife and wants to be really, really close, his thoughts send an impulse to his nerves and arteries. This causes the spongy tissue of the penis to fill with blood and to become hard and straight in preparation for intercourse.

"The wife's desire for her husband causes her body to get ready, too. Her vagina gets softer and more relaxed and begins secreting a lubricating substance. This will make intercourse more comfortable for both partners.

"The husband places his penis into his wife's vagina. Their bodies fit together just the way God designed. The couple enjoys the way their closeness feels, because it's something special, just for the two of them.

"As the husband and wife begin to move their bodies together in harmony, each feels very pleasurable sensations. A sense of excitement grows and grows, and may reach its peak in what's known as an orgasm or climax. During orgasm the husband ejaculates. That means that sperm forcefully move from his penis to his wife's vagina. This is accompanied by good feelings for the man and does not cause his wife any discomfort. In case you're wondering, sperm and urine never pass at the same time.

"The wife doesn't ejaculate, but she may also reach orgasm. Her emotions are just as intense, just as pleasing as her husband's.

"After ejaculation, the male's penis begins to return to its original state, which is soft and limp. Both marriage partners are filled with a feeling of total relaxation, warmth, and love for each other. This may be where the term 'making love' came from, because sexual intercourse between marriage partners does make their feeling of love for each other seem new all over again. They remember all the other times like this, all the years they've shared a life together—the good times and the not-so-good times. And they feel as if they truly are 'one flesh'—an inseparable unit.

"Of course, it's possible for a male and female to have sexual intercourse without any love at all. It can be just two bodies coming together. But that's not what God had in mind when he made us.

"One of the best things about a couple's sexual relationship is that no matter how many years they're married, they can still want each other sexually. They can still find great joy and satisfaction in their sexual relationship. Sexual intercourse between husband and wife is one of God's best gifts to human beings.

"It may take a couple some time to make their sexual relationship work as it should. Even when the bride and groom love each other very much, it sometimes takes a while until they become tuned-in to each other, until sexual intercourse is completely enjoyable for both of them."

Explaining Orgasm

Help! My teenager wants to know what an orgasm feels like. How do I explain it?

Depending on the age of your teenager, you may wish to say something like this: "There's nothing I could say that would really tell you how an orgasm feels, because it's different for each person. One doctor says it's like a sneeze, and that's probably as good a comparison as any.

"You know how you feel when you have a sneeze coming on? How your whole body seems to be concentrating on the sneeze and you can't even think of anything else? And then after you've finally sneezed, you feel relaxed and peaceful? That's a bit like an orgasm. During sexual intercourse, a person's whole body is tensed up in anticipation, and then there's a sort of explosive feeling, just as a sneeze is an explosion in your nose. And then you feel warm and good and relaxed and peaceful all over."

Talking to Teens about Responsible Sexuality

My teenager seems so sophisticated that I feel awkward talking about the dangers of premarital intercourse. What can I say?

Young people often try to appear knowledgeable about sex, especially around their parents. For one thing, they may feel self-conscious. For another, they may be sure they'll be in for a long lecture, perhaps packed with parental emotion. So the first rule is this: Try not to preach. Allow the youngster to express opinions, and don't betray surprise or shock or make judgments. For if you do, your child will neither hear what you say nor respond.

You've probably already discussed sexual intercourse and the basic facts covered in Chapter 6. You may want to briefly discuss them again and then take it one step further. A key concept that young people will usually accept is that of personal responsibility. There's a lot of ground to cover, and you may wish to say any of the following, which may fit a given occasion:

"Maybe you've begun to feel something special about one person in particular. When you begin to care about someone, you just naturally want to be close—to touch and hold that person. And when these feelings become very strong, you may very much want to have sexual intercourse with that person. God put that desire into us; He made us sexual beings. And He invented marriage as the special relationship in which a husband and wife are to have sexual intercourse.

"Having intercourse with someone outside of marriage is a sin against God and the other person. No matter how someone may try to make it look right, intercourse outside of marriage comes down to people putting their own pleasure first—before obedience to God or before the deeper relationship of love that God intended marriage to be.

"In marriage, a man and a woman promise to love each other, to care for each other, and to be faithful to each other—for life. Then they establish a home of their own—and they're proud of it. They don't have to make excuses to anyone. Best of all, they have plenty of time to learn how to have a good, satisfying sexual relationship.

"You see, it's more than a couple getting into bed together and WHAM!—it's dynamite!—the way it happens in the movies. Even for most married couples it takes time to develop a satisfying sexual relationship—for some a few weeks, for some several months. And for some it may take a year or more.

"The point is, married couples know they have time to work it out. They know that their partner isn't going to walk out and find someone else just because their sexual adjustment is taking a while. They've committed their lives to each other, so they have the freedom to be themselves.

"Their commitment also means they're ready to be responsible for whatever comes—to care for each other when sick, to support each other emotionally and financially—and to take the responsibility of a child if the wife becomes pregnant.

"Ever since you had your first menstrual period (wet dream), you've been physically able to become a mother (father). Maybe the idea of having a baby of your own sounds exciting to you—or maybe it sounds ridiculous. In any case, it's always a real possibility for a couple having intercourse—even when they practice birth control.

"You've probably heard about some of the different kinds of birth control. Some of them are the condom, which fits over the penis; the diaphragm, which fits over the entrance to the uterus and must be fitted by a medical professional; various kinds of vaginal tablets, foams, and creams. There is also the birth control pill, which a woman must get by prescription and follow the prescribed dosage. Regular checkups by a medical professional are advisable, to monitor for any harmful side effects.

"In 'natural family planning' methods (the only method recognized by the Roman Catholic Church), a woman closely keeps track of her monthly periods, avoiding intercourse during those times each month when she is most likely to get pregnant.

"Sometimes young people think that if they use birth control, they can have sex at any time. 'After all,' they may say, 'why not? We're not hurting anyone and there won't be a baby.' So they may have intercourse first with one person, then with another, and they think this means they're free, liberated—grown-up.

"But there is no way to avoid the chance of pregnancy except to avoid intercourse. Nothing else is 100 percent foolproof—not even the pill. Not even if the male withdraws his penis before ejaculation, because there's often an early leakage of small amounts of sperm long before he ejaculates.

"So, for all practical purposes, every time a couple has intercourse, they should be ready to assume full responsibility for a child. Most young people are far from ready for that. Even if they really love each other and decide to get married because they are going to have a baby, it's not easy. Too many things make it tough.

"The young husband usually has to quit school to take a low-paying job and may never finish his education, so he's stuck with less income all his life. The young wife is twice as likely to die from the complications of pregnancy. Her baby is two or three times as apt to die during its first year than if she were an adult. Their marriage is much more likely to end in divorce, too, than if the same two people had married in their 20s, when they were more mature.

"Perhaps you're thinking the girl could always get an abortion. It's true that abortions are much more available than they used to be. Sometimes you hear people say that an abortion is just a simple little procedure, that it's all over in a few minutes and all your problems are behind you. But it's not that easy.

"For one thing, an unborn baby is more than just 'a problem' or an inconvenience. It's a real human being (Psalm 139). Killing it is killing a human being. Also, a woman who has an abortion, even when she seems calm and levelheaded and quite casual about the whole thing, often suffers emotional trauma that cause a lot of serious problems in the future—maybe even affect her ability to relate to her husband later on. Once she's had an abortion, a woman may have trouble with future pregnancies, too, when she and her husband may want a child very much.

"Another factor to recognize is the prevalence of sexually transmitted diseases, especially among young people. Despite what you've heard, latex condoms do not ensure truly 'safe sex.' One reason is that condoms do not cover all of the genital area of either partner. Several of the sexually transmitted diseases can by transmitted by bodily fluids, even when a couple avoids sexual intercourse. So if a couple has only mouth/genital contact (oral sex), or anal sex, or even just rub their sexual organs together without actual penetration, the infected partner still can transmit an STD.

"Many of the drugs that were hailed as miracle cures a few years back don't do the job anymore because bacteria have developed a resistance to them. Besides, several of the sexually transmitted diseases give no sign at all that one is infected. So a young man or a young woman may be infecting everyone with whom he or she has intercourse and never even know it.

"Worst of all, STDs can cause permanent damage, so that when people marry and want to have children, they may find that an STD has made them sterile. And we're not even talking about AIDS, which can lie dormant in your body for more than 10 years before you even test positive.

"So you see, these sexual feelings you're having now have many implications. It's not nearly so simple as it sounds. When people talk about the sex drive and how we must satisfy it, they aren't considering the whole person and the emotions involved. Sometimes it almost seems as if they think people are just sex organs with a body attached.

"But God gave us a conscience, a brain, and emotions as well—love and caring and self-control. 'Self-control' sounds almost out-of-date, but it's still valid. Self-control does no damage to either male or female. But giving in to our sexual urges outside of marriage does, because it's a sin. A better term for you and me as Christians would be 'God-control,' for He has promised that we can lean on His strength no matter what the temptation.

"Now that you're becoming an adult, more and more you are making your own decisions. Sometimes that can be difficult, but you're not in this alone. Christ died to free you—and me—from being slaves to behaviors that are wrong, as the Apostle Paul reminds us:

> *Don't you know that when you offer yourselves to someone to*
> *obey him as slaves, you are slaves to the one whom you*
> *obey—whether you are slaves to sin, which leads to death, or*
> *to obedience, which leads to righteousness? (Romans 6:16).*

"Lots of young people—and adults, too—think that sex outside of marriage is sophisticated. But following others' behavior isn't half so worthwhile or satisfying as being strong in Christ. Because when we choose to follow His teachings, we have inner peace. And that's one of the best things in life.

"You know, our loving Heavenly Father wants us to have the best! Young people who follow His guidelines come into marriage *free!* Free of guilt, free of fear that their bodies may harbor an unknown virus or bacteria of a sexually transmitted disease. Free of hurtful memories that rob them of joy. Such brides and grooms give each other a priceless wedding gift: their hearts and minds and bodies, free of scars from the past or fear of the future.

"Isn't that what you want for yourself? Won't it be wonderful to be able to *give* that gift on the day you marry?"

Note to Parents

All this information is for *you*—for background. You'll want to present it in your own words, your own way. It's easy to make this sound like a sermon. That's almost guaranteed to make your young person stop listening. Strive to make this a dialog; along the way, ask what your teenager thinks about what you're saying. If there's a disagreement at times (and there probably will be), don't judge or scold. Talk about both viewpoints and try to be objective.

Most of all, point to the Scriptures and to Christ, the authority Christians accept in all matters—even for sexual values. Note how, for example, in 1 Corinthians 6:12–20, St. Paul urges God's love for us in Christ as the reason and the power for Christians not only to abstain from immorality but to grow in fulfilling their God-intended sexuality. In searching Scriptures like these together, be warm and caring; communicate that you know your youngster's feelings because you've struggled with them, too. Emphasize that sexual feelings aren't in themselves wrong. Rather, as good gifts of God, they're a potent force that should be wisely used at appropriate times in a person's life—to God's glory.

Should Parents Give Teenagers the Pill?

My friend is giving her teenage daughter the birth control pill. She says she knows the girl will be having intercourse anyway and it would be terrible if she got pregnant. She maintains that all parents should face reality and do the same, because it's the lesser of the two evils. Is she right?

This may be a fairly common practice today, but your friend's logic is faulty. It's not inevitable that teens will be sexually active; many choose not to be. When a parent gives a child any kind of birth control device, several things happen—all negative:

- The parent is, in effect, saying, "Of course you will be sexually active" and thus implies approval.
- There is no principle of values or of sexual restraint to which the teenager can aspire.
- For the teens who want to avoid sexual activity, this adds one more pressure. Not only the world and their peers but also their parents are "pushing" early sex. They may well decide, "What's the use of fighting it?"

- Once sexual activity has begun, there is an ongoing temptation to become careless in using contraception.
- Remember that the birth control pill not only provides no protection against sexually transmitted disease, it actually increases a female's vulnerability. Feeling secure against pregnancy, teenage girls feel no need for any other protection.

Teenage sexual activity is a fact of life, and of course young people should have thorough sex education and a knowledge of birth control. As parents, we should counsel with our teens, keep the lines of communication open, and try to instill the desire to live a Christian life. That includes giving them our matter-of-fact expectation—our trust—that they'll live by our family standards—and God's. Surely that is a more positive approach than handing out birth control products.

The Pap Smear Test

When should girls start having them? How often?

The Papanicolaou, or Pap Smear, is a laboratory test to determine whether there are any abnormal cells on a woman's cervix, which could signal the possibility of early malignancy. In doing this test, the doctor uses a long cotton swab to take a small specimen of cells from the cervix (the mouth of the uterus).

Because this test is valuable in spotting cancer in its beginning stages (when it can be much more easily cured), most doctors recommend that every woman, beginning in her late teens, have a regular Pap smear. The doctor will advise how often to repeat the test. If a woman is taking birth control pills or is on hormone therapy, most physicians insist on regular vaginal examinations and more frequent Pap tests.

Sexually Transmitted Disease/Venereal Disease

I hear a lot of talk about STD—is that the same as VD? I need some basic information.

STD is the current and more precise term for what was formerly called VD. Both refer to diseases that are sexually transmitted. The list is long, but we all need to know the facts. And it's important to help our children understand, so they have truth rather than rumor. Here, in alphabetical order, is a rundown on STDs.

AIDS *(Acquired Immune Deficiency Syndrome)*

AIDS was identified in the U.S. and in Europe in 1981. First identified mainly among homosexual men and then intravenous drug users, AIDS has spread into the heterosexual population. AIDS is caused by the human immunodeficiency virus (HIV). Once the virus invades the body, it silently begins to ravage the immune system. The HIV virus invades the bloodstream, attacking white blood cells, and also cells of the bone marrow, spleen, liver, and lymph glands. These cells normally manufacture antibodies against disease and cancer, so the HIV-infected person becomes increasingly vulnerable.

During the incubation period (which can be more than 10 years), the infected person may be unaware of infection and display no identifiable symptoms. Nevertheless, the individual is capable of transmitting the virus all along. Testing only establishes that the infected person has finally produced enough HIV antibodies to show up on the screening. From that point on the individual is declared "HIV positive."

Compare that fact to confident statements frequently expressed in the media. Mutual HIV testing is touted as the "guarantee" that two individuals can fearlessly engage in sexual activity. Not so! Test results are valid only for the time the test was taken—not the next week or the next month. For all these reasons, some health professionals consider AIDS a "ticking time bomb." There simply is no way to estimate the number of infected persons, male or female, straight or gay, married or single, young or old.

Presently no vaccine exists, mainly because the virus keeps mutating. (At least one other HIV strain has been identified in several countries.) In recent years, pharmaceutical researchers have developed several new approaches to treatment. These new drugs reduce levels of HIV in the bloodstream and seem to slow or halt the advancement of AIDS. Cost of treatment is very high. Different combinations of drugs are being used, with varying degrees of success. The earlier such treatment is administered, the better. Rarely, a patient may appear to become HIV-free, but to date it's uncertain whether the virus actually is eradicated or simply has become dormant.

Some HIV-positive persons have lived with their status for a number of years; a few even have reverted to negative tests. But they remain infected with the AIDS virus, nevertheless. Intensive research and trials of numerous other treatments continue, but so far none offers a cure. Without future medical breakthroughs, an HIV-infected individual eventually will test positive for HIV/AIDS. Whether new treatments will prevent such infection from progressing to full-blown AIDS and/or prove truly lifesaving remains to be seen.

Is AIDS contagious? How is it spread?

Although AIDS is contagious, it can't be spread in the same way as the common cold, chicken pox, or measles. Rather, it's contagious in the same manner as are other sexually transmitted diseases such as gonorrhea or syphilis. In fact, research suggests that other sexually transmitted diseases and genital ulcers actually promote the transmission of AIDS. It's thought that these conditions provide an entry route for the HIV or somehow alter the immune system.

After infection with the AIDS virus, some people remain apparently well. Nevertheless, these persons can transmit the virus to others through sexual relations; through sharing needles in intravenous drug use; or when donating blood, organs, tissue, or sperm. AIDS is spread through blood, semen, and vaginal secretions. During sexual activity, invisible breaks may occur in the skin of the rectum, penis, or vagina, allowing passage of the virus. Other possible (though far less likely) avenues are the mucous membranes of the eyes, nose, and mouth, which are permeable and thus allow viruses to pass directly into the bloodstream.

The AIDS virus has also been identified in menstrual blood, tears, saliva, sperm, and feces. It's presently considered unlikely that the virus can be transmitted by any means other than sexual contact or by blood exchange.

After studies of families who lived and interacted with AIDS patients, the following are accepted as fact:

- AIDS is not spread by casual contact in school or on the job.
- AIDS is not spread by crying, coughing, sneezing, or by ordinary social kissing. ("French" kissing, or wet kissing, may be an exception.)
- AIDS is not spread by swimming in pools, bathing in hot tubs, or eating in restaurants, even if restaurant workers are carrying the virus.
- AIDS is not spread by shared towels, shared bed linens, or shared eating and drinking utensils.
- AIDS is not spread by mosquito bites, other insect bites, or pets.
- AIDS is not spread via toilet seats, doorknobs, or telephones.
- Standard heat sterilization measures, responsibly performed

according to accepted guidelines, have been found to destroy the virus.

Now let's look at how the AIDS virus is spread.

- AIDS is spread by sexual contact: penis-vagina; penis-rectum; mouth-penis; mouth-vagina; mouth-rectum. (Tiny tears in the rectum commonly occur during anal sex, providing the virus easy access. In the mouth, minute breaks along the gum line or in the cheeks allow the AIDS virus direct route into the blood.)
- Since 1986, the U.S. Centers for Disease Control and Prevention have recommended that couples not kiss deeply if one of them is infected with the AIDS virus, mostly because of the possibility of mouth lesions or bleeding gums.
- AIDS is spread through sharing intravenous needles and syringes such as those used for "shooting" illicit drugs.
- AIDS is spread from mother to child during pregnancy, while giving birth, or when breast-feeding. With each pregnancy, the HIV infected woman has a 25 percent to 33 percent chance that her baby will be born HIV positive. Some infected children remain healthy for several years, while others have a much shorter life span.
- AIDS may be spread through the use of any unsterilized skin-piercing instrument, including needles used for ear piercing or tattooing. Disposable needles are safest. The same cautions apply to any instrument that may touch blood, semen, or vaginal fluids of an infected person.
- AIDS may be spread via razors or toothbrushes, which could allow passage of the virus directly into the bloodstream through a break in the skin and/or gums.
- AIDS has been contracted by some health care workers who came in contact with the blood of AIDS patients through puncture accidents, or by being in a situation where blood squirted into their eyes, mouth, or through breaks in their skin.
- Since 1985 the blood supply has been considered virtually safe. (Those who had blood transfusions or received blood products prior to that have been considered at risk, as was anyone who had sex with such an individual. By now enough time has passed that the time of risk likely has passed.)

Note: You cannot contract the AIDS virus by donating blood, since sterile needles are always used.

Which people are most vulnerable to HIV/AIDS?

At highest risk are those individuals who currently—or in the past—engage(d) in the following:

- homosexual or bisexual activity
- intravenous drug use, especially with unsterilized needles, or when using needles shared with another person
- sex with multiple partners
- sexual activity with prostitutes, many of whom both "shoot" drugs and have multiple sexual partners
- sexual partners of persons who indulged in the above

These individuals play Russian roulette with their very lives, by choice. But so do their spouses and sexual partners, often unknowingly. The majority of women who develop HIV/AIDS are wives and lovers of infected men. In fact, health officials have verified a number of AIDS cases where HIV infection followed just one exposure to the HIV virus through sexual activity. Truly when you have sexual intercourse with another person you are, in effect, having sex with every person with whom your partner has ever had sex.

Does anyone ever test positive when not HIV infected?

Occasionally false-positive test results do occur. An individual who fits in none of the risk categories may be tested by employers or donate blood, then receive the "HIV positive" verdict. So it's vital to remember that laboratories make mistakes and that flu shots, pregnancy, and other factors occasionally cause the false-positive reading. Rather than waste time in needless panic, immediately go for retesting. Physicians, community hospitals, and county agencies perform HIV tests.

My teenagers say, "Use a condom and there's no danger!" Are they right?

"Safe sex" is being sold—in schools, in the media, by government spokesmen. But how safe is it really? Here are some factors to consider:

- Condoms can break, leak, or be used improperly. In pregnancy prevention, respected sources list the actual failure rate at 10 to 14 percent (14 pregnancies out of 100 occasions of sexual intercourse). Yet because of the menstrual cycle, a female can become pregnant only a few days of each month. The HIV/AIDS carrier, however, can transmit the virus 365 days of the year.
- The U.S. Food and Drug Administration randomly tests condoms for leaks during the manufacturing process but the U.S. govern-

ment regulations allow four condoms per 1,000 to have holes discernible by testing equipment.

- An FDA study tested latex condoms and determined that 32 percent of normal intact condoms leaked enough HIV-sized particles to arouse concern. The other 68 percent of the condoms leaked "only a few." (Based on this study, the Centers for Disease Control announced that latex condoms "are an effective mechanical barrier to fluid containing HIV-sized particles.")
- The condom must be worn every single time, from the very beginning (foreplay) until the end act of intercourse, since the male typically releases a small amount of semen long before ejaculation. (According to the CDC, this includes oral or anal sex as well. The failure rate is highest with anal sex.)
- Spermicides and other forms of birth control do not protect against AIDS, although those containing nonoxynol-9 were partially effective in laboratory tests. (By the way, spermicides are not totally effective against other STDs either.)
- It's considered prudent for the female to wear a diaphragm plus spermicide even when the male wears a condom.
- An American Medical Association study of AIDS transmission among couples in which one partner was infected was reported in their publication. Over the 18-month period studied, the HIV virus was transmitted to the uninfected partner in 17 percent of the couples who used condoms.
- During a conference of 800 professional sex educators, counselors, and therapists, the question was posed: Would any among them personally engage in sexual intercourse with their known HIV-positive "dream" partner, depending on a condom for protection? Not one person raised a hand.

It sounds as if it's impossible to escape AIDS!

Not at all! Although AIDS is often termed a "modern plague," there's an important difference compared to, for example, the black death. Unlike plagues of the past, AIDS is a preventable disease. A spokesman for the Public Health Service says, "AIDS is not a plague that strikes people for no reason, but a disease that strikes people whose behavior allows them to be infected."

The "AIDS epidemic" remains largely confined to homosexual men and intravenous drug users, their sex partners, and their children. Clearly, AIDS does spread heterosexually. The number of females, sex partners of infected males, continues to rise. But studies indicate that total numbers attributable to heterosexual spread remain relatively small. Whether that will change is anyone's guess. Given the long incubation period and the short history of HIV/AIDS, it's simply too early to be sure.

Certainly our children are growing up in a more dangerous world than we did. Therefore, it's important that we know the truth in order to help our young people separate fiction from fact. Knowledgeable parents can hold their own when countering false assurances. The goal is not a scare campaign, but a healthy fear, since teens typically believe "It couldn't happen to me." After all, if they swallow the story of "safe sex," they gamble their lives. Teens are also subject to peer pressure, and experimentation with sex and drugs is rampant today.

Young people need more than facts and fear if they're to be strong from within. Worldly wisdom proclaims, "Here, take a condom. Everybody knows you'll have sex sooner or later." Teens need a reminder that God made them more than a helpless bundle of hormones. Let's replace threats or guilt trips with the vivid picture of God's best for them. Let's add frequent expressions of confidence that we know they wouldn't endanger that wonderful future just for a few moments of self-indulgence. And let's lovingly tell them the truth.

For there is a way to be safe—at any age! The old virtues, as delineated in the Bible, are the "new" wisdom of our time. Chastity before marriage, absolute faithfulness within marriage, avoiding practices that could be harmful to our own bodies or to other individuals— these are the guidelines laid down by today's health authorities—and by our loving God so very long ago. Medical personnel, Christian or not, would agree that this is the only truly "safe sex."

Our Creator laid out the way to His best—the monogamous, life-long sexual relationship He designed for wives and husbands. But God's plan provides more than safety. Such a marriage relationship ensures a secure framework of mutual trust in which wives and husbands together can freely express and enjoy their sexuality.

Chancroid

This STD hasn't been much of a factor since the late 1940s. However, in the past few years, reported cases have increased sharply, and it is once again being regarded as a significant disease here, as it already is in many parts of the world. Chancroid is a bacterial disease that causes genital ulcers and swollen lymph glands. The usual treatment is sulfonamide drugs, although erythromycin may be used. If not treated, the disease can destroy the urinary tract and other body tissue.

Chancroid usually is found among heterosexuals, with 3 to 25 times more cases among men than women. The higher ratio is in outbreaks involving patrons of prostitutes, probably because just a few women can infect many men, and because the women are hard to locate.

Chlamydia

This "silent sexual disease" is a leading sexually transmitted disease in the U.S. today. One state health department estimates that new cases of this bacterial infection are about four times more common than new cases of genital herpes or genital warts *combined*. Approximately four million new cases of chlamydia occur each year. Most physicians do *not* routinely test for it.

Symptoms often are mild, mimicking other ailments. Typical symptoms in females are abdominal pain (sometimes with fever), vaginal discharge, difficulty in urinating, and pain during sexual intercourse. Likely symptoms in the male are urinary tract infections (urethritis) plus a discharge from the penis, which contains no pus. About 70 percent of women and 30 percent of men display *no* symptoms at all, so the disease quietly ravages the body.

Consider these dismal facts. The prevalence of chlamydia is highest among sexually active women under the age of 20. Left untreated, chlamydia can spread throughout the reproductive tract, causing infertility or sterility in both women and men. Officials identify chlamydia as the culprit in an estimated 40 percent of the country's cases of pelvic inflammatory disease (PID), an infection that can permanently scar the uterus and fallopian tubes. Chlamydia is now labeled a major cause of infertility among women of childbearing age. Usually the infected woman is unaware of the damage until she wants to become pregnant.

When women with chlamydia do conceive, their chances of an ectopic (tubal) pregnancy increase dramatically. An ectopic pregnancy is fatal to the fetus, and life-threatening to the mother as well. If a normal pregnancy occurs, and the woman is not treated during gestation, the baby can be infected while passing through the birth canal. These infants may develop eye, ear, or lung infections. Following delivery, an infected woman is at greater risk of uterine infection.

Risk of chlamydia increases with multiple sex partners. Chlamydia is curable with antibiotics such as tetracycline (not penicillin). Since the disease is easily passed back and forth between partners, physicians advise that both be tested and, if necessary, both be treated.

Genital Herpes

Genital herpes is a very contagious viral infection, occurring around the sex organs, spread almost entirely by sexual contact. Most genital herpes infections are caused by herpes simplex type 2 virus, which is related to herpes simplex type 1, the virus involved in chicken pox, fever blisters, and cold sores. (There are other herpes viruses, as well, that cause other conditions.) Estimates by various agencies range from five to 30 million individuals in the U.S. who are infected with genital herpes, with at least 300,000 new cases each year. (Physicians are not required to report the disease.) According to some studies, 30 to 40 percent of single, sexually active people are infected.

Genital herpes usually begins within four to seven days after infection, but symptoms can begin as long as a month later. A mild burning or tingling in the genitals and buttocks often signals an outbreak. Fever, flu-like symptoms, and swollen lymph nodes in the groin may follow. Within a week, fluid-filled blisters appear, which then break and form raw, extremely painful sores. For males these outbreaks usually are confined to the penis, scrotum, and buttocks. In females, however, both external and internal sex organs are involved. About one-third of herpes patients experience only mild symptoms such as itching, redness, and a few insignificant bumps, or no symptoms at all.

But the majority of those infected face recurring outbreaks for life. Severity and frequency of these flare-ups vary with the individual, but usually are less severe than the initial infection. Herpes sufferers typically have from one to six outbreaks per year. Triggering factors are individual, too—anything from a cold to menstruation to emotional stress to wearing clothes that fit too tightly. Doctors can prescribe acyclovir, which may speed healing during flare-ups and help prevent recurrences. (Pregnant women should alert their physicians before taking acyclovir.)

Formerly it was thought that herpes transmission was possible only during an active period, when open sores are present. New research indicates that about 70 percent of those with genital herpes contracted the disease from a partner with no noticeable symptoms. In the absence of symptoms, doctors have difficulty diagnosing genital herpes. Blood tests currently are not definitive, and are not a guarantee in any case. Viral cultures are more reliable.

Herpes infections can be spread whenever any part of one's body (or one's partner's body) touches active sores containing the virus. Mucous membranes (as in the mouth or genital area) are especially vulnerable. When the skin is broken, as from cuts, eczema, and abrasions, risk of infection increases dramatically. If there are sores in the mouth, using saliva as a wetting agent for contact lenses can transfer the herpes virus to the eyes. Should the virus invade the eye, it can cause lesions on the cornea that may result in partial or complete vision impairment.

During outbreaks, keep sores clean and dry, and don't pick at them. Frequent hand washing is a necessity. Avoid touching your eyes. Be extra careful around babies, and avoid kissing them. Suspend kissing and sexual intercourse until all lesions are healed. Wash hands frequently during active outbreaks, but don't share towels.

Note to Women

Be aware that the herpes virus can cause miscarriage and stillbirth. During delivery, the mother may pass the virus to her baby, especially if she has open sores, so it's essential that the physician carefully monitor the pregnant woman's condition. Many physicians insist on a Caesarean delivery to minimize the hazard for the child. If the mother has herpes, the newborn's pediatrician should be informed. Despite prompt identification and treatment, those infants infected with herpes are at great risk of developing brain damage or dying.

It's also vital that females have Pap smears annually. Herpes infection is lifelong and multiplies the woman's risk of developing cancer of the cervix. Cervical cancer is curable, but early detection is essential.

Is there anything else I should know about herpes?

The herpes virus can lie dormant in the body for years, usually in nerve tissues, without producing symptoms. Although it doesn't survive for long outside the body, recent data suggest that the virus can live for several hours in warm, moist areas such as wet towels, and perhaps on some other surfaces. So although the virus is killed by normal washing of glasses and cutlery, it seems prudent to avoid sharing them. That would make it wise, also, to forego sharing towels and clothing of the person with active herpes. This information would explain those cases where the herpes patient vows he or she has not engaged in any sexual activity, yet develops genital herpes. Toilet seats are considered safe. Yet it's at least theoretically possible that a person whose genital lesions are "weeping" might leave some serum on the toilet seat that could then contact the skin of the next user. Infection is unlikely, because the amount of drippage would be small. Still, covering the seat with toilet tissue or using a seat cover would offer extra protection.

Genital Warts (Venereal Warts; Condyloma; HPV)

The extensive human papilloma virus (HPV) family causes genital warts, as well as warts on fingers and plantar warts on the soles of feet. In the U.S., HPV infection has reached epidemic proportions, estimated at more than one million new victims each year and 24 million who now have the disease.

An individual may be infected with HPV viruses and be able to transmit genital warts sexually long before symptoms develop. Venereal warts often are painless. Ranging from pinhead size to a quarter inch in diameter, warts may be invisible to the naked eye. The growths can be raised and bumpy, or flat, or shaped like a tiny cauliflower. Color may vary from white to gray to pink to brown.

In females, warts may form on the cervix, in the vagina or rectum, on the vulva or anus, and sometimes in the urethra. Lasting irritation of the female organs is a frequent after-effect of HPV. Males most commonly develop warts on the penis, but also on the scrotum, the anal area, and the urethra.

Venereal warts can be difficult to detect, even by physicians. About 70 percent of women with external warts also have warts on the cervix or in the vagina. Pap tests often provide the first clue. Internal lesions typically go unnoticed, but sometimes itch and bleed. Warts may be treated with acidic chemicals. Another treatment is a prescription cream, from a class of drugs called immune response modifiers. Genital warts also can be removed surgically, treated with cryotherapy (freezing), or with laser therapy (vaporizing with a high-powered light beam). Early treatment is most effective, when warts are small. Repeat treatments often are necessary, either because infected cells remain, or because virus that was hidden deeper in the skin later emerges. To date, treatment can eliminate the warts, but the virus remains in the body, and warts often reappear.

During an outbreak of condyloma (warts), caution should be exercised. Scratching genital warts can spread them to other parts of the body. Sexual activity should be avoided until warts are completely gone. To break the back-and-forth of HPV transmission, the partner of an infected individual should be checked, and if necessary, be treated at the same time as the patient.

A prospective mother who's at risk for genital warts needs to be tested early in her pregnancy. Mothers with genital warts can deliver babies with warts. In rare cases, venereal warts enlarge during pregnancy, actually blocking the birth canal, making Caesarean delivery a must. Avoid chemical treatment of warts during pregnancy, since it can damage the unborn child. Cryotherapy, however, is considered safe.

Condyloma usually is spread by sexual contact. Other possible routes of infection include contaminated surfaces around hot tubs and jetted tubs, poorly sanitized commercial suntan beds, and towels used by persons with genital warts. Individuals may harbor the virus for years, developing symptoms only when their immune systems are challenged by other conditions.

The Cancer That's Contagious

Many medical authorities believe that nearly all cancers of the cervix, vagina, and vulva are associated with human papilloma virus infection. Studies show that sexually active young women under age 16 are much more likely to develop cervical cancer if exposed to HPV from male partners. (Not all warts, however, cause cancer.) An individual can be infected with both benign and malignant cancer-causing genital warts. Presently only a Pap test and/or biopsy can determine the presence of precancerous cells or the beginning of actual cancer, although other tests are under development. Since cervical cancer is highly curable in its early stages, regular Pap tests are a must.

Penile cancer is quite rare, but it's on the rise, too. Once again, the blame is laid on the growing number of sexually active persons infected with condyloma. According to one study 60 percent of male partners of women with warts were also infected. If an infected female is treated, but her infected partner is not, she will be reinfected.

Sexually active teens and young adults form the largest group of those with venereal warts. According to one study, as many as 40 percent of sexually active teens are infected with HPV. This predisposes females to develop cancer of the cervix later. Not surprisingly, the likelihood of developing genital warts increases with multiple sex partners, and also with the presence of other STDs. Women taking birth control pills statistically are at a greater risk of condyloma, presumably because they're less likely to insist that their partners use condoms.

Some authorities believe that smoking also boosts the chance of developing genital warts, although reasons are unclear.

Gonorrhea

Over one million new cases of gonorrhea occur annually. Gonorrhea is a serious bacterial infection that is spread only through sexual contact, and up to 90 percent of females who have intercourse with an infected male contact gonorrhea.

The usual incubation period is two to seven days, but symptoms may not appear for weeks, months, or years. Up to 80 percent of infected women display no symptoms and unknowingly become carriers, capable of transmitting gonorrhea to their sexual partners. It's less likely that infected men will be symptom-free.

Symptoms may be mild or severe. A typical symptom in infected individuals of either sex is painful urination. Males may notice a cloudy, pus-like discharge from the penis. Females with gonorrhea may have a cloudy vaginal discharge, possible lower abdominal discomfort, or abnormal vaginal bleeding. Gonorrhea can also infect the mouth or rectum as a result of oral or anal sexual contact.

Left untreated, gonorrhea usually involves a man's entire reproductive tract. Impotence may result. Untreated gonorrhea in the female may infect the uterus and surrounding abdominal area, leading to pelvic inflammatory disease and/or peritonitis. Frequently the end result is sterility. In both sexes, when gonorrhea goes undetected and untreated, it can spread throughout the bloodstream, infecting the heart, the brain, the joints, bones, tendons, skin, and other parts of the body. When an infected, untreated woman gives birth, her baby's eyes are subject to infection with the gonorrhea bacteria.

The causative bacteria have become increasingly resistant to standard antibiotics, so the newer medicine cetriaxone is recommended. (Since it's quite common for infected females also to have chlamydia, that should be treated with tetracycline.) Use of a condom is considered protective. However, it's important to avoid sexual relations until treatment has cleared up the symptoms, as shown by a follow-up culture. One reliable source estimates that in the U.S. each year as many as 100,000 women are rendered sterile by gonorrhea and the pelvic inflammatory disease that almost always follows.

Pelvic Inflammatory Disease (PID)

A sexually active female teenager is much more susceptible to *all*

STD germs, but especially PID. An unchecked STD—usually chlamydia or gonorrhea—is the standard cause of pelvic inflammatory disease. However, E. coli and other bacteria also can be at fault. Some sources consider intra-uterine devices (IUDs) a risk, since when the physician inserts the IUD, bacteria unavoidably gain entry. (To a lesser extent, medical procedures that dilate or open the cervix, abortion, miscarriage, or childbirth can increase a female's vulnerability.) All it takes is for the causative organism to move through the vagina and invade the woman's reproductive organs.

The type and severity of PID symptoms depend on the type and strength of the infecting bacteria. General symptoms include moderate to severe pain in the lower abdomen; fever, either high or continuing low-grade; nausea, which may include diarrhea and vomiting; painful intercourse; unusual vaginal discharge; spotting and/or pain between menstrual periods; change in normal menstrual periods—irregular or unusually long periods, heavy bleeding or discharge, or painful periods.

Pelvic inflammatory disease is an acute infection, and medical treatment is needed at once. Antibiotics are standard treatment, sometimes with complete bed rest or hospitalization. The health care provider will prescribe abstinence from sexual intercourse until both partners have finished prescribed medication. Follow-up visits are mandatory, so that the doctor can be sure no germs or infection still linger. (In case of adhesions and abscesses within the pelvic cavity, or should antibiotics not eliminate pain, surgical intervention may be necessary.)

All this is needed because too often, irreparable damage is PID's legacy, particularly with repeated episodes. Fallopian tubes become scarred, then completely blocked. Infertility, even permanent sterility, frequently results. When pregnancy does occur, the chance of the fertilized ovum attaching inside the tube is high (ectopic pregnancy). When this happens, death of the fetus is inevitable, and risk to the mother's life is high.

Syphilis

Syphilis is at a 40-year high, with about 150,000 new cases every year. Add to that about 3,500 cases of congenital syphilis in babies born to infected mothers. Each year brings a dramatic increase in both types. Spread mainly by sexual contact, syphilis is one of the most serious STDs, causing widespread tissue damage. After infection, an individual with untreated syphilis becomes a carrier, able to infect sexual partners for up to four years. About 50 percent of those who engage in sexual activity with a syphilis carrier will become infected.

This disease is more effectively controlled with antibiotics than most other STDs, although the causative bacteria have shown increasing resistance to drugs. Even when treated, syphilis can erupt many years later. Since it progresses more slowly than gonorrhea, there is time for treatment and for alerting contacts of patients. Within 10 to 40 days—but sometimes as late as three years—after sexual contact with a diseased person, a lesion appears, usually in the anal-genital area. This is a small, red, elevated sore (chancre) that becomes moist and eroded. After four to ten weeks the sore will heal without treatment.

Women may show no symptoms. However, diagnosis can be made by a physical examination and blood test anytime following the first three weeks after contact. (Before that the tests usually don't reflect the presence of infection.)

Now comes the secondary stage. The internal damage begins, and the diseased person is still contagious. The person may develop non-itching eruptions or a rash, usually on the trunk of the body, commonly within six weeks to three months. There are other symptoms, usually only distinguishable by a competent physician.

The latent period then arrives, with no symptoms, and the person is not contagious. However, the late stage of syphilis may show itself in any organ—the brain, the central nervous system, the cardiovascular system, and on the skin. These late effects, which can be disabling, crippling, and disfiguring, may not arrive for more than 30 years.

A pregnant woman infected with syphilis usually transmits the disease to any child conceived during the first two years of the illness. If she is treated during the first four months of pregnancy, the child is generally not infected. The child of such a mother may show signs of congenital syphilis later—up until puberty and even as late as age 30.

By the way, contracting syphilis once and then being treated for it does not confer immunity. A person can be reinfected again and again.

A condom lessens the chance of contracting syphilis. Spermicide, diaphragms, and other contraceptives offer no protection.

Vaginal Infections

Some vaginal infections are acquired sexually, but many are not. All can be passed from the female to the male, then back again, so physicians often prescribe treatment for both. Let's look at the most common types.

Monilia (also known as "yeast infection" or "Candida")

Normally, the acid level in the vagina keeps fungus growth in check. Body chemistry changes can raise the likelihood of a yeast infection, which results from an overabundance of yeast fungus. With monilia, the vaginal discharge is thick and white ("cheesy"). Itching is intense. Pain during urination or sexual intercourse is common. A health care provider should make the initial diagnosis, to be sure the cause is monilia. The usual treatment is with antifungal suppositories or creams available over-the-counter. (Ask the physician whether treatment is available for the male sexual partner as well.)

It bears mention that monilia is very common among women. Many consider it chronic, because it tends to recur. Technically this is not a sexually transmitted disease. However, a female with a yeast infection can pass it to her partner and vice versa.

Trichomoniasis (also known as "trichomonas vaginitis" or "trich")

Trichomoniasis is caused by a microscopic, one-celled organism known as a trichomonad, which can survive for several hours on articles such as damp towels and swimsuits. Nevertheless, this infection almost always is acquired through sexual intercourse. The vaginal discharge may be greenish or yellowish, either watery or frothy and usually with an unpleasant odor. Vaginal soreness, persistent itching or burning are typical symptoms. A physician can prescribe an oral medication, probably metronidazole, for both sexual partners. Be sure to report any side effects.

Bacterial Vaginosis (BV)

Several types of bacteria (including gardnerella) can cause this infection. Vaginitis usually is transmitted sexually, but not always. The vaginal discharge, often heavy, is watery and has a strong "fishy" odor. If vaginal itching and burning are present, another infection may be present. Metronidazole is the usual prescription. To avoid reinfection, both male and female sexual partners need treatment.

Talking It Over

Faced with the appalling statistics on AIDS and other sexually transmitted diseases (STDs), many of us would like to take our children and go find a nice, safe, deserted island somewhere. Nevertheless, we needn't cower in fear, either for our children or for ourselves.

Society is in a mess because of wrong choices that bring unpleasant consequences. The encouraging news is that all of us—at any age—can by the power of God's Spirit make wise choices that bring good results. Kids need to hear that. Even very young children watch TV ads designed to frighten viewers into altering sexual behavior that can lead to death from AIDS.

So it's important to provide a warm, loving atmosphere in which out children can voice their fears and questions. Use your own judgment as to how detailed your answers will be; you know your own children better than anyone. Give enough information to convince them that STD is not to be taken lightly.

When talking with your children, take the positive approach. Remind them (and yourself) that in almost every instance, infection with STDs and with AIDS is the result of sexual relations with an infected person, or of using contaminated needles during the use of illicit intravenous drugs. These are avoidable hazards. Step 1 is for the individual to decide to say no.

Our task as parents, then, is to foster that decisiveness and strength—and self-confidence—in our children. That means speaking frankly about choice-and-consequence, but also frequently reminding them of who they are in Christ. The good news of God's forgiving love through Jesus gives power to be what God has made us to be in Christ— His children. The apostle Paul tied it all together when he said:

> Flee from sexual immorality. All other sins a man commits
> are outside his body, but he who sins sexually sins against his
> own body. Do you not know that your body is a temple of the
> Holy Spirit, who is in you, whom you have received from
> God? You are not your own; you were bought at a price.
> Therefore honor God with your body
> (1 Corinthians 6:18–20).

Yet how are Christians to respond when all around us are people who blatantly disregard God's principles for living?

God forgives all sin; we know that. But He doesn't excuse sin. Rather, He calls people to repent of their sin—also sexual sin. We're living with the aftermath of the sexual revolution. What was so highly acclaimed and prized has been revealed for what it is—the grim bondage of health and emotional problems that can last for life—or end, too soon, in death.

God forgives—freely, mercifully, and unconditionally. The fact that human beings live with the natural consequences of unwise choices doesn't nullify God's forgiveness and acceptance of the repentant sinner. As parents, we need to convey this message also—with love, not as a threat, not to inspire fear. Choices and actions yield consequences; that's simply the way life is. There is, as they say, no free ride.

Perhaps the trend of public opinion is beginning to turn in that direction. Certainly it's unexpected that "the world" would echo biblical principles. Yet some experts have summed up their advice in familiar-sounding principles: Say no to drugs and to sex outside the marriage relationship and you are also saying no to AIDS, STD, and unwanted pregnancy.

But because saying no can be very difficult, we need to stress something else, too, with our children. As Christians we're not alone in our struggle to withstand the pressures and temptations of living. The "reinforcing rod" in our will is God's Holy Spirit. Paul passes on specific assurance:

> No temptation has seized you except what is common to man. And God is faithful; He will not let you be tempted beyond what you can bear. But when you are tempted, He will also provide a way out so that you can stand up under it (1 Corinthians 10:13).

Following God's guidelines, we—and our children—can live in confidence, not fear. Moved by our own absolute forgiveness in Christ, we can confront and accept each other in love, not judgment. And as Christians we can rejoice together in the inspired word of Scripture that remains fresh and up-to-date in every age.

Abortion

My teenager says that abortion is simply "termination of an unwanted pregnancy" and that women have a right to exercise control over their own bodies. I don't agree with her, but how can I counter what she says?

Legal abortions are widely available. In many states, teenagers can obtain a legal abortion without the consent or knowledge of their parents. Community free or low-cost clinics may enable teenagers to obtain such services even though they're financially dependent on their parents.

Medically speaking, abortion is a simple procedure if done within the first trimester (three months) of pregnancy. Some people consider abortion a means of birth control (which it is in many countries) or at least as an alternative to birth control if conventional methods fail.

However, abortion is not an option for the Christian. The reason can be found in verses such as these:

You created every part of me; You put me together in my mother's womb. ... When my bones were being formed, carefully put together in my mother's womb, when I was growing there in secret, You knew that I was there—You saw me before I was born (Psalm 139:13, 15–16 TEV).

When Elizabeth heard Mary's greeting, the baby leaped in her womb, and Elizabeth was filled with the Holy Spirit (Luke 1:41).

Typical fetal movement would not likely rate recording in Scripture. That baby leaped for joy in his mother's womb when she was in the presence of the pregnant Mary, the mother of Jesus Christ. The baby in Elizabeth's uterus grew up to be John the Baptizer, who was appointed by God to prepare the way for His Son.

These verses leave no doubt that the fetus is a human being—with a soul—before birth. Doctors tell us an individual's gender, color of eyes and hair, body build and height, potential intelligence, talents and abilities, and many other characteristics of body and spirit are determined at the moment of conception. Although the embryo is but a half-inch long 28 days after conception, its brain is already growing, its internal ear and eye structures are formed, its heart is formed and beating, and it has a simple digestive system, a functional circulatory system, kidneys, and liver. All this refutes the argument that an embryo or a fetus is simply a "clump of tissue" or merely "potential life."

Abortion can have a detrimental effect on the future life of the female. Subsequent pregnancies may be seriously affected because there's a greater likelihood of miscarriage or premature delivery. (This effect is intensified when the female is a teenager.) In addition, many women who obtain abortions suffer psychological and emotional trauma, either at the time of the abortion or later, and this may continue for long periods of time.

For Christians and for all serious-minded people, abortion can never be taken lightly. For it is God who has given human beings the ability to become parents—the gift of being partners with Him in the wonder and mystery of new life.

God has given us the privilege and responsibility of caring for our body, but not absolute ownership of it:

Do you not know that your body is a temple of the Holy Spirit, who is in you, whom you have received from God?

You are not your own; you were bought at a price. Therefore honor God with your body (1 Corinthians 6:19–20).

Nor has God awarded us the power over the life of another human being—not even ourselves:

In His hand is the life of every creature and the breath of all mankind (Job 12:10).

The question of how to deal with an unplanned pregnancy, whether you are married or single, old or young, is never simple, although prevailing public opinion may make it appear so. As Christians, however, we're in the world but not of the world. We are "the people of God" (1 Peter 2:10). Our allegiance—our responsibility—is to God. Thus no matter what may be the situation with which we wrestle, we view it from that perspective:

For in Him we live and move and have our being (Acts 17:28).

But what if it's too late? The fear was too strong, the faith too weak ...

Many Christians who have chosen abortion have later regretted it with all their hearts. Whether you had the abortion yourself, or whether the aborted fetus would have been your grandchild, realize that this sin, too, went to the cross with Jesus Christ. Your pain may endure, but your guilt should not! Ponder these wonderful truths:

If we confess our sins, He [Jesus] is faithful and just and will forgive us our sins and purify us from all unrighteousness. ... He is the atoning sacrifice for our sins, and not only for ours but also for the sins of the whole world (1 John 1:9; 2:2).

Therefore, there is now no condemnation for those who are in Christ Jesus, because through Christ Jesus the law of the Spirit of life set me free from the law of sin and death. For what the law was powerless to do in that it was weakened by the sinful nature, God did by sending His own Son in the likeness of sinful man to be a sin offering (Romans 8:1–3).

So lay down your burden and allow yourself to be free of it. If the one involved in the abortion is your child, speak your own forgiveness and affirm God's marvelous grace. For if you've carried this load, your child has, too.

There Is an Alternative to Abortion; Give Life!

When faced with the fact of a teenage child who either is pregnant or has fathered a child, Christian parents anguish over what to do, how to proceed. As already discussed, abortion is the killing of human life, so that's not an option. Marriage is no longer viewed as the logical solution.

It may be obvious to all that the pregnant parents are immature. Perhaps the reluctant father has left, or the two young people are not now (and never were) sure they love each other. To marry and make a home would be meaningless and futile, for if they're not ready for marriage, divorce looms as a likelihood, compounding the pain and the problems.

Christians ask, "What would the Lord want us to do? What would be the best for the majority of those involved? What is *right*?"

If the pregnant teenager carries her child to term—then what? Sure, unmarried teens bring their babies to school, and celebrities tout the joys of having a baby without the bother of having a spouse. Supportive grandparents can help—or even raise the child. But grandparents need to be sure that they're joyfully willing and ready to begin again. The question is, Would this be best for the grandchild?

Another possibility exists. The girl could make a plan for adoption for her baby. Difficult? You bet—for everyone involved. But such an act of sacrificial love would bring something wonderful out of sin and heartache. The child would enter a secure home with two loving parents. In many cases, truly this would be placing the good of the child first.

For those faced with this dilemma, it's important to seek the counsel of one's pastor and/or a reliable counselor. Whatever is decided, repercussions will last a lifetime, so spiritual guidance and an objective viewpoint are mandatory.

Homosexuality

What do I and my child need to know about homosexuality?

Despite endless research and debate, one question likely will continue unanswered: Is homosexuality a choice or an inborn characteristic—like the color of one's eyes? The "homosexual community" has become a powerful force in U.S. society, with some kind of mention almost daily in news media. Open discussion and display, "Gay Pride" marches, frequent news reports, etc. appear to prove that homosexuality is a growing lifestyle. Yet some recent data and more accurate interpretations of older research suggest that the actual number of gays in the U.S. is a much smaller percentage of the population than previously supposed. Controversy rages as to the verifiable totals.

The Bible speaks clearly against homosexual behavior. However, it's important to differentiate between homosexual behavior and homosexual persons. As Christians we seek to reach out in love to those persons who have homosexual tendencies, recognizing them as fellow sinners. Knowing our Father's warm love ourselves, we seek to pass it on.

Yet as parents we pray that our children will avoid the obvious pain of being homosexual. We watch as openly gay and lesbian actors portray openly homosexual characters—the lead characters in movies, TV shows, and books. We see homosexuality being presented as just another lifestyle choice, as typical and acceptable as Mom-and-Dad-and-two-kids. We suspect (or know) that school sex-education classes echo the same theme and praise "diversity." And we're uneasy. Will all this exposure somehow lead our own child into the homosexual life? Counselors say that almost never happens.

Still, parents may look at a small-boned son and fear he's not "masculine enough." Or a daughter who lacks the feminine graces, who always showed a preference for typically male activities, may cause her parents to wonder whether there is "something wrong" with her.

Such ideas are stereotypes. For example, adult male homosexuals are in "masculine" fields such as engineering, in management-level jobs, in professional sports, and in positions of public trust.

Surely our children are more aware of the subject than ever before. Sometimes they question themselves. With typically immature judgment they may recall scattered episodes of homosexual play when they were growing up and may question their own sexuality. So it's good to mention casually that such happenings are normal, especially among young boys, and do not indicate latent homosexual tendencies.

Young people need reassurance and acceptance from us, not reinforcement of their own doubts. For instance, we may wonder whether our daughter spends too much time with her girlfriend or whether our son hangs around with the guys too much. Whether we voice these concerns openly or not, our attitudes will almost surely come through. The message our youngsters will pick up is "I'm not sure about you." Some young people go to great lengths to prove they're heterosexual, with disastrous results.

So how can we help our children to forge a strong, balanced self-identity? How can we foster healthy sexual attitudes?

1. First, last, and most important, we put our major effort into achieving a mutually satisfying, mutually supportive marriage

relationship. This gives our children a healthy pattern of male-female interaction. We love each other and our children—and it shows. If we have problems we can't handle, we seek help for the good of our children as well as ourselves.

2. The parent of the other sex tries to be emotionally stable, caring, and loving toward the child.

3. The parent of the same sex is strong but also warm and tender, so the child can have a good relationship and wish to identify with that parent.

4. We accept our children and their gender. We do not attempt to make a girl into a substitute boy, or vice versa. Neither do we push them into stereotypes.

5. We accept our children as they are, even when they disappoint us in appearance or performance. And we speak our love frequently.

6. We let our children know we're there to help with their problems. We listen to their stories with enthusiasm. We reassure and encourage them every chance we get.

If we follow these principles, our child will feel accepted as a person and will have the confidence to develop healthy relationships. Certainly there are fine Christian parents who've discovered their child is homosexual. Some believed their home life to have been a model of Christian love and respect. When their child "comes out," they are shattered, disbelieving. What are they to do?

Their task is the same as any other parent's: love their child with the love only Jesus Christ can give, and pray for their child's welfare. For it's precisely when our children are most vulnerable, when they know and we know our own pain, that Christ calls us to let His love shine through the cracks in our self-perception. Loving the sinner does not mean we love the sin. But if our children become uncomfortable around us, if the bond between us breaks, we won't be able to together acknowledge our human sinfulness and celebrate God's forgiveness in Jesus.

Premenstrual Syndrome (PMS)

When it's "that time of the month," I'm hard to live with. How do I explain PMS to my teenage daughter?

PMS won't kill you—but for some women (and their families) this condition makes life extremely unpleasant every month. Symptoms begin 7 to 14 days prior to the menstrual period and usually stop when menstruation begins. Symptoms may include breast swelling and tenderness, nervousness and irritability, headache, fluid retention, increased or decreased sex drive, digestive disturbances, dizziness or fainting, acne outbreaks, and depression.

Severity of symptoms may vary a great deal from one month to the next, and some women are never affected. The cause is fluctuations in the circulating level of hormones (especially estrogen and progesterone) and blood chemicals. These variables increase sodium retention in the bloodstream, which causes edema in body tissue and in the brain. Theories of treatment also vary greatly. Many authorities recommend exercise, along with reducing salt, sugar, and caffeine intake. Nonprescription PMS medications are available, as are standard pain medications. (It's considered safe to simulate prescription-strength ibuprofen by taking 800 mg every 6 to 8 hours.) Effectiveness varies among users. Some women find that everyday intake of extra calcium and magnesium is helpful. Physicians can choose from an array of drugs such as natural progesterones; diuretics for water retention; antianxiety medications; and various hormonal (or antihormonal) agents.

The Basics of Birth Control

Please talk a bit about the newer methods of birth control.

First a dose of reality. Recently a long-established research group in the field of contraception announced its findings on how often the most-used contraceptives fail. Here's the breakdown:

	In Theory	In Reality
Birth Control Pill	1%	6%
Latex Condom	2%	14%
Diaphragm	3%	16%
Spermicides	3–8%	26%
Rhythm Method	2–10%	16%
Sponge	10%	18%

Implants (Norplant)

Norplant comes in a set of six capsules that contain synthetic progesterone and are surgically implanted under the skin of the upper arm. Once in place, they prevent pregnancy for five years, and can be removed at any time. The hormone released is similar to the amount released daily by the progesterone-only birth control pill. Studies show that Norplant allows only four to five women per thousand to become pregnant per year, making it the most effective method that's reversible. Costs for Norplant vary widely, but it's a one-time charge, plus the fee for removal.

Norplant's biggest drawback is that about two-thirds of users have light to moderate unpredictable bleeding. After one or two years, that drops to one-third who experience bleeding. Currently there is some controversy concerning the removal of the implants. A few women have claimed that extraction of the implants left ugly scars. Apparently the implants had embedded themselves in the skin, making removal more difficult than anticipated.

Depo-Provera

This synthetic progesterone is given by injection and suppresses ovulation for 14 weeks. Doctors recommend a 12-week schedule, just to be sure. Estimates of effectiveness range from 0.3 percent to a rate similar to the birth control pill. Depo-Provera causes irregular bleeding at first. After a year, 80 to 90 percent of users have no menstrual periods.

Intrauterine Devices

The IUDs presently approved for use in the U.S. are considered safe. In typical use the failure rate ranges up to three percent. They must be inserted by a physician. The greatest risk of infection occurs at the time of insertion, since bacteria inevitably are introduced into the uterus. Usually the woman's body eliminates the bacteria shortly.

In the past, IUDs have been associated with pelvic inflammatory disease, which can cause infertility and/or sterility. Since there's a small chance of infection with even newer IUDs, women who plan to become pregnant in the future may want to weigh carefully whether or not to use one.

———————— **Things Teens Wonder About** ————————

Size of Penis

Is a guy's penis ever too big (too small) for the woman?

Just as people come in all different shapes and sizes, sexual organs do, too, and each one is normal for that person. It really doesn't make any difference what size and shape penis a man has; he can still be a satisfying sexual partner for his wife.

As for the woman, the vagina is made to stretch, so it will accommodate any size of penis. This stretching doesn't hurt the wife; it's perfectly normal and the way God made females.

Does a wife enjoy it more if her husband's penis is bigger?

No, because the sensitive areas of her body are mostly on the outside and in the area around the vaginal opening. Therefore she'll be sexually stimulated just as well if her husband has a smaller penis.

Does it hurt the woman when the man inserts his penis?

If the female is frightened or nervous or feels guilty, she may tense her muscles all over, including the vaginal opening. When this happens, she may feel some discomfort. Also, when she's feeling this way, the lubricating process within the vagina doesn't seem to work as well so the combination of the two may cause some difficulty. That's another reason why intercourse works best within marriage; the couple feels secure and can relax.

Circumcision

Does circumcision make sex better for the man?

So far as authorities can tell, the sensitivity of a man's penis is not affected by circumcision. Nor does it seem to make a difference for the woman. However, it does make it easier to maintain cleanliness. Removal of the foreskin prevents the accumulation of a discharge called smegma, which can develop an objectionable odor.

Intercourse during Menstruation

Will it hurt the woman if a couple has intercourse while she's menstruating?

There's no physical reason why a couple should not have intercourse during the female's menstrual period. It is not painful for her. However, she may feel self-conscious. Or either partner simply may feel that lovemaking is too messy because of the menstrual discharge. Each husband and wife must decide for themselves, depending on their own personal feelings.

Young Adults:
Ready to Fly

When I was a child, I talked like a child, I thought like a child, I reasoned like a child. When I became a man, I put childish ways behind me (1 Corinthians 13:11).

Maturity. Wisdom. Faith. We all want our young adult offspring to possess these wonderful qualities, don't we? All along, our goal as parents has been to equip them to fly on their own—to be wise, well-balanced Christians adults. We confidently expected that by this point in their lives we'd be seeing the results—the fruit—of all those years in which we labored and learned and grew together.

Not necessarily.

Many young adults go through an interim phase when they seem to turn their backs on everything they've seen and heard in their families. This is the time of life when our children cut the emotional cords with us and strike out on their own, often living by values with which we disagree. During this period, parents ask, "Where did I go wrong?" As the months and years crawl by, we torture ourselves with, "Will they do a U-turn?" Perhaps we even start to hear familiar Scripture promises as accusations.

So it's important to remember that this breaking-away stage is a necessary step in the development of the self-functioning adult. It can be a period of distress for both parent and child. Parents see all the years invested in raising their children—who were and probably still are the central focus of their lives—and wonder what is left. All too often the parent panics and attempts to hang on desperately.

This practice can take many forms. Some parents refuse outright to let a child go away to college, for instance. "I had my heart set on going to a school 100 miles from home," said Kristen, "but Mom and Dad said that they thought it best that I live at home and go to the junior college. Who did they think they were kidding, anyway? I knew the real reason. If they'd been honest, they'd have admitted they just couldn't stand to see me leave home. I should think they'd be glad to get me out of the house and be alone for a change.

"I guess if I were a really good daughter, I'd want to live at home, but the truth is I resent being forced to stay and I get out of the house at every opportunity. I just want a chance to be on my own. Yet when I start talking about it, Mom goes off to bed with one of her sick headaches and Dad looks upset. Then I feel so guilty I just give up. I guess I'll be here till I'm 35!"

Such manipulation is often unconscious on the part of the parent; we all tell ourselves, "It's for their own good!" and we can find a dozen reasons to prove it. But underneath we fear being alone, dread change, feel anxious that the new stage of life that looms ahead may be an empty one.

A Right to Their Own Lives

It's well to remind ourselves again that we don't own our children. They're people in their own right, with the obligation and privilege to make decisions and solve problems for themselves. (However, if we note actions we know to be without doubt against God's will, we have a duty to speak as one concerned Christian to another.)

"When my daughter became an adult, I didn't know how I should talk with her," said Rachel. "For a while I just skirted around issues that bothered me—figured it was none of my business now. But I began to realize we're still united in Christ, so I 'rushed in where angels fear to tread,' as they say, afraid Kelly would get angry.

"I managed to stay low-key. Used lots of 'I' messages—like 'I'm really concerned because I'm afraid you'll be hurt' or 'I'm uneasy because I wonder if you've thought about how that stacks up against your Christian values.'

"Once in a while I slipped up and started the old line: 'Kelly, you should …,' but I'd catch myself and start over," said Rachel, smiling. "Actually, these turned out to be some of the best talks we've ever had! Although Kelly didn't seem too impressed at the time, she made some changes later that showed she didn't just resist my viewpoint out of hand."

Rachel learned a valuable lesson for Christian parents. Relating to grown children is most effective—and most harmonious—when we accept and respect our young people. We can still be their valued friends, still listen, still offer occasional counsel, but as one adult speaking to another. Our active parenting is over. Future shaping will come mostly from God and the sometimes-painful experiences of living.

They're Living Together!

Parents realize, even though young people seldom do, the anguish that awaits those folks who make foolish life choices. Living together without marriage falls in that category for most parents because of the physical, emotional, and spiritual risks involved. It's particularly distressing for Christian parents when our children accept the world's value system.

"When Callie moved in with Jose, I just couldn't accept it," said Annette. "I know and she knows that God's Word speaks against sex outside of marriage. Rick and I have always had a happy marriage, always told our kids there's nothing better, that it's worth waiting for. We thought they agreed with us. Then Callie went off to school, and the next thing we knew, she was living with Jose.

"It's been months, yet I still lie there in the middle of the night and think about all my failures as a parent. It seems all my thoughts begin with 'If only ...' I can't get it out of my mind. I just know she's ruining her life! And how will she pick up the pieces after this affair breaks up? What if she gets pregnant? Or even picks up AIDS? Rick and I never thought a child of ours would be living in sin, and we're not coping very well. I just don't know what to do. ..."

Most of us would have many of the same feelings. Although the situation itself troubles us, the openness, the fact that such couples seem almost to flaunt their relationship, troubles us even more.

Over and over we rehash the dilemma, wondering what course of action is best. In the end, we have no real choice but to accept the fact that these young adults are accountable for their own actions. Like us, they must live with the natural consequences.

This doesn't mean we remain silent. Rather, as adult Christians we'll speak the truth in love. We'll be honest about our feelings (the "I" messages again). For if we try to cover them, pretend they don't exist, our child—who knows us so well—will sense them anyhow.

On the other hand, belaboring our objections is counterproductive. For if we lay down conditions, if we force our child to make a choice between us and the "live-in," we may put up walls that last for years. Whether we like it or not, the fact is that we can't force our adult child to adopt our own Christian values system. But we can continue to pray for him or her—and continue to demonstrate our love and caring, standing by to help and give counsel if asked.

We need to turn to God's forgiveness in Christ, too, for our failures as parents. All of us have made mistakes, of course, and would be far wiser parents the second time around. But there is no second time.

We did the best we could with the wisdom and maturity we had. It serves no purpose, either for us or our children, to dwell on what we should have done. Rather we can rest on our gracious God's promise to use even our blunders and omissions for good (Romans 8:28).

And Then They Were Married ...

When a child marries, parents often breathe a sigh of relief. Even if there are doubts about a prospective child-in-law, they may well feel that marriage is preferable to living together or possible unwed pregnancy. Now the young adult is establishing a legal, separate family unit. Society, the church, and we ourselves pronounce our blessing.

But we may not yet be ready to give up control of our children, to let them function as adults whose major commitment must be to their marriage. Debbie, for instance, feels she has the right to walk into her son's home unannounced. "Why not?" she says. "Mark is still my child! Why should I have to telephone first? And why bother to knock when I have a key? After all, I'm not a stranger, I'm family!"

But her daughter-in-law doesn't see it quite that way. "We never know when that door is going to open," says Renee. "This is our home, but we have no privacy. And she expects us to spend every Sunday afternoon at her house. Honestly, Mark's mom must think she owns us! I know she means well, but we have our own lives to live.

"And she asks the most intimate questions—inquires about our 'adjustment' and are we 'having any problems.' We know what she means, of course, but I'm not going to discuss our sex life with her. And boy! do we feel pressure about having a baby!"

No couple should feel it is their duty to supply their parents with grandchildren. This has to be a decision a couple reaches because they sincerely want children. We may dream of becoming grandparents, or even feel a marriage isn't a marriage without children. But our own children are the ones who will face the very real demands of parenthood.

If and when they do become parents, we'll want to respect our children's rights as parents. The way they choose to bring up their children is up to them.

It's Their Decision

In short, the whole subject of relating to grown children, married or unmarried, could largely be summed up in three words: It's their decision. Hard to accept, isn't it? Yet that's exactly what we wished for ourselves when we were young—the freedom to run our own lives, to make our own choices, to be respected as adults.

Our relationship with our grown children is a fragile thing, like holding a tiny bird in our hand. If we hold too tightly, it will die. But if we treat this living thing kindly and show love, if we set it free to follow its own leading and fly its own journey, it will come back of its own free will. Then we'll have a friend for life—one who chooses to have a relationship with us.

Surely such friendship must be the best possible reward for all the years of parenting!

Forgiveness Begins Right Here

The trouble with rearing children is that by the time we know what we're doing, we're all done! As usual, hindsight is 20/20. We say to ourselves, "Oh, if only I could go back and start all over!"

But we can't. We did the best we could with what we knew at the time. Of course, we know more now. We're experienced!

So this is the day to confess our failings and receive God's absolution. Each of us is the product of our own upbringing. Our parents had their own particular hang-ups, and we patterned our own parenting after theirs. We can't go back. We can only begin where we are. If our children are younger, we can simply fill in what we've omitted and pick up from there. If they're teenagers or older, we'll want to openly admit our failures and do what we can to reopen the door to communication. Forgiveness and acceptance can flow between us, even now.

But then we put it behind us. We all survived our less-than-perfect parenting, and our children will, too. If we have had a loving relationship with our spouse and/or served as a good role model, we've already done the most important thing.

Still, what if we feel we've failed even at that?

Then we do what God has told us to do with all our cares. We cast them upon Him and leave them there. We rest in the certainty that Christ totally paid for these sins, too, when He died on the cross and rose again. We trust His grace and power and love to transform our failures into good in the lives of our children—in His way, in His own good time. We accept our children and ourselves as fellow redeemed sinners.

And then we move on to the next phase of living, forgiven and free to be the best woman or man we can be, enjoying our own sexuality. For at any age we are sexual beings.

God planned it that way.

And as He said when He created the first male and female: "It [is] very good"!

Pictorial References

Female External Sexual Organs

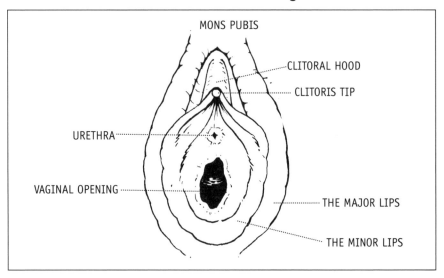

Male External Sexual Organs

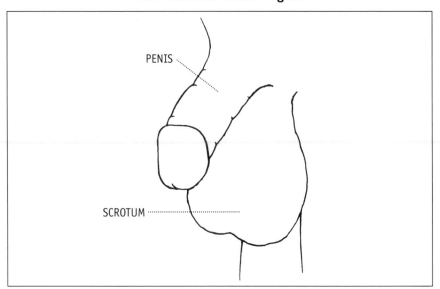

Female Internal Sexual Organs

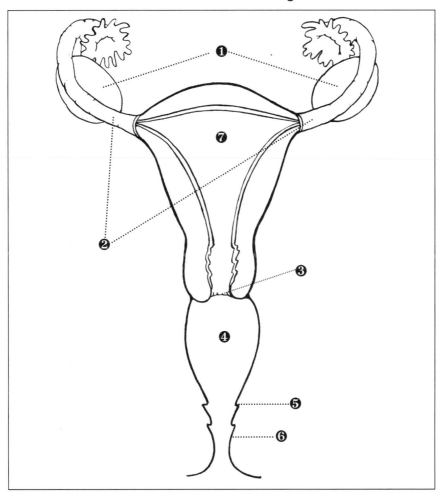

1. Ovaries
2. Fallopian Tubes
3. Cervix
4. Vagina
5. Hymen
6. Inner Labia
7. Uterus (Womb)

Male Internal Sexual Organs

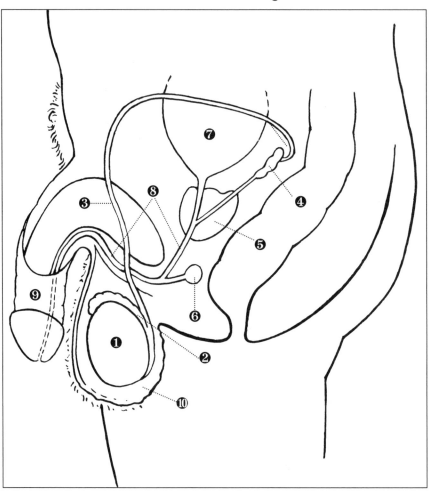

1. Testicle
2. Epididymis
3. Vas Deferens
4. Seminal Vesicle
5. Prostate Gland
6. Cowper's Gland
7. Bladder
8. Urethra
9. Penis
10. Scrotum

Early Development of the Fertilized Egg

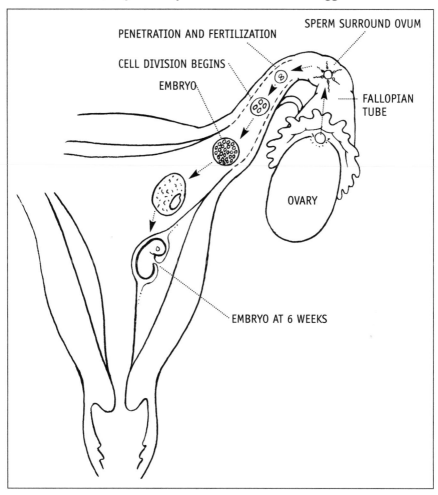

PENETRATION AND FERTILIZATION

SPERM SURROUND OVUM

CELL DIVISION BEGINS

EMBRYO

FALLOPIAN TUBE

OVARY

EMBRYO AT 6 WEEKS

Vasectomy

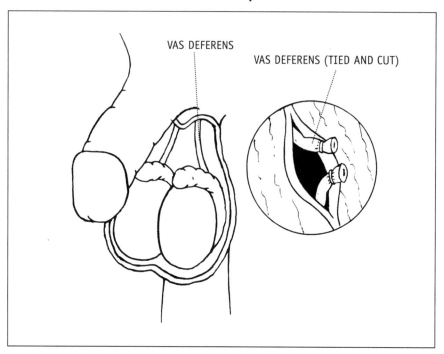

VAS DEFERENS

VAS DEFERENS (TIED AND CUT)

Tubal Ligation

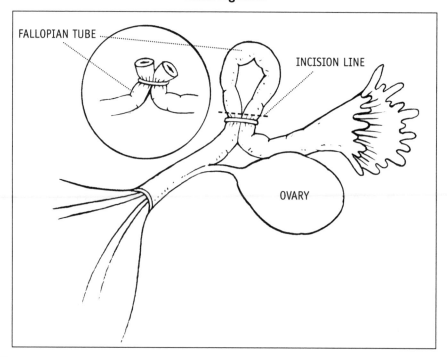

FALLOPIAN TUBE

INCISION LINE

OVARY

Glossary

Abortion (a-BOR-shun) The premature termination of a pregnancy. There are three types:

Voluntary. A procedure performed at the request of the pregnant woman.

Spontaneous (miscarriage). A natural termination usually due to some abnormal development of the fetus.

Therapeutic. A medically recommended procedure prompted by abnormal developments that threaten the life of the mother and/or the fetus.

Some common methods of induced abortion:

D & C (Dilation and Curettage). A medical procedure in which the cervix is dilated and a spoon-shaped surgical instrument called a curette is used to scrape the lining of the uterus. Used during the first 12 weeks of pregnancy.

Hysterotomy. A major surgical procedure in which the fetus is removed through an incision in the abdomen. Used only after 12th week of pregnancy.

Menstrual extraction (regulation). Extracting the lining of the uterus (normally part of the menstrual process) by a suction technique; normally done within two weeks after a missed menstrual period, before positive diagnosis of pregnancy can be made.

Morning-after pill. Prescription drug taken by the woman in a single dosage after sexual intercourse to prevent implantation of a fertilized egg.

RU-486. Prescription medicine taken by the woman to detach the embryo from the uterus. See Note, under Contraception.

Saline abortion. A saline (salt) solution is injected into the woman's uterus, causing abortion to occur spontaneously. Used only after 14th week of pregnancy.

Vacuum curettage. After dilation of the cervix, suction is used to empty the uterus. Can be used up to the 12th week of pregnancy.

Abstinence (AB-stin-ens) To voluntarily avoid. In sexual connotation, to refrain from sexual intercourse.

Acne (AK-nee) A skin condition characterized by pimples, blackheads, and/or excessive oiliness. Common in adolescents.

Adolescence (ad-uh-LES-sens) The period of life between puberty and adulthood.

Adultery (a-DULL-ter-ee) Sexual intercourse with a person who is legally married to someone else. The term is often used to describe any sexual intercourse outside of marriage.

Afterbirth See Placenta.

AIDS (Acquired Immune Deficiency Syndrome) Life-threatening viral disease. Transmitted through exchange of blood and/or semen, either by sexual contact or by use of dirty or shared needles when shooting intravenous drugs. May also be the result of receiving contaminated blood products. Average incubation time from infection is 8 to 10 years. At this time, AIDS is fatal.

Amniocentesis (am-nee-o-sen-TEE-sis) A procedure whereby a sample of the amniotic fluid surrounding the fetus is drawn and analyzed to detect possible birth defects.

Amnion (AM-nee-on) The thin membrane that forms the sac of liquid surrounding the fetus within the uterus. Contains amniotic fluid, in which the fetus is immersed for protection again shocks and jolts.

Anal Sex (AY-nal) Sexual relations where the penis is inserted into the rectum.

Anus (AY-nuss) The opening at the base of the buttocks through which solid waste is eliminated from the intestines.

Areola (a-REE-o-la) The dark tissue around the nipple of the female breast.

Artificial Insemination A medical procedure whereby semen is injected into the vagina close to the cervix by artificial means. It can sometimes enable pregnancy in spite of fertility problems.

Birth Canal See Vagina.

Birth Control Technically, the control or prevention of birth, regardless of method. Commonly used to refer to contraception and/or contraceptive methods (the prevention of conception by use of devices, drugs, or other means).

Birth Control Pill See Contraception.

Bisexual (by-SECKS-shoo-al) Having both male and female sex organs. Commonly used term for describing a sexual interest in both sexes.

Bladder (BLAD-er) A sac in the pelvic region where urine is stored until elimination.

Breech Birth The birth position when the baby's feet or buttocks appear first instead of the usual (headfirst) position.

Caesarean Section (si-SAIR-ee-an) (Caesarean Birth; "C" Section)

Delivery of a baby by surgical incision through the abdomen into the uterus.

Candidiasis (can-dih-DYE-a-sis) Inflammation of the vagina caused by a yeast-type fungus (*candida albicans*). Commonly referred to as a "yeast infection."

Castration (kas-TRAY-shun) Removal of the sex glands—the testicles in men, ovaries in women.

Cervix (SER-viks) The narrow, lower part of the uterus, that opens into the deep portion of the vagina.

Chancre (SHANG-ker) A small sore or ulcerated area, usually on the genitals, that is the first symptom of syphilis.

Chancroid (SHAN-kroyd) Sexually transmitted bacterial disease. Causes genital ulcers and swollen lymph glands. If left untreated, can damage urinary tract and destroy other tissue.

Change of Life See Climacteric; Menopause.

Chastity (CHAS-ti-tee) Abstention from sexual intercourse.

Chlamydia (kla-MID-ee-ah) Sexually transmitted bacterial disease. Can cause pelvic inflammatory disease and infertility.

Chromosome (KRO-mo-soam) One of the more-or-less rod-like bodies found in the nucleus of all cells, contains the heredity factors or genes. 22 pairs of chromosomes account for a person's hereditary characteristics. The 23rd pair determines sex. See X Chromosome and Y Chromosome.

Circumcision (ser-kum-SIZH-un) Surgical removal of the foreskin or prepuce of the penis. Originally a Jewish rite performed as a sign of reception into the faith; now generally performed for purposes of cleanliness.

Climacteric (kly-MACK-ter-ik) The time of physical and emotional change—the end of menstruation in women and a lessening of sex-hormone production in both sexes. See Menopause and Midlife Crisis.

Climax See Orgasm.

Clitoris (KLIT-or-is) A small, highly sensitive female organ located just above the urethra.

Coitus (KO-i-tus) Sexual intercourse between male and female, in which the penis is inserted into the vagina.

Colostrum (ko-LAH-strum) The nourishing, thin, milky fluid secreted by a woman's breasts just before and after she gives birth.

Characterized by high protein content thought to contribute to the child's early immunity from infectious disease.

Conception (kon-SEP-shun) (Impregnation) Penetration of the ovum (female egg cell) by a sperm, resulting in development of an embryo—new life.

Condom See Contraception.

Condyloma (kon-di-LO-ma) See Genital Warts or Sexually Transmitted Disease.

Congenital (kon-JEN-i-tal) Existing from birth. May or may not be inherited.

Conjugal (KON-ji-gul) Pertaining to marriage: e.g., conjugal love.

Continence (KON-ti-nens) Exercising self-restraint, particularly regarding the sex drive.

Contraception (kon-trah-SEP-shun) (Birth Control) The prevention of conception by use of devices, drugs, or other means. Commonly used methods:

Birth control pill. A contraceptive drug made of synthetic hormones that prevent ovulation. Available only by prescription and must be taken as prescribed.

Cervical caps (SER-vih-kal). Prescription item, barrier method of contraception, fits over cervix. Long used in Europe. Similar effectiveness to diaphragm, but said to be less irritating and can be left in place for longer period.

Condom (KON-dum). A thin rubber sheath placed over the erect penis before intercourse to prevent the sperm from entering the vagina.

Contraceptive sponge. Nonprescription, disposable, polyurethane sponge, two inches in diameter, fits over cervix. Comes presaturated with spermicide (nonoxynol 9), which is activated when moistened with water prior to insertion. Effective for 24 hours, including multiple acts of intercourse. Very slight risk of toxic shock syndrome.

Depo-Provera (DEH-po pro-VAIR-ah). Synthetic progesterone, given by injection, that suppresses ovulation for 14 weeks.

Diaphragm (DIE-ah-fram). A thin rubber disc that covers the cervix and prevents sperm from entering the uterus. Must be initially fitted by a doctor.

Norplant. Set of six capsules (rods) containing synthetic progesterone, surgically inserted under skin of a woman's upper arm. Suppresses ovulation and changes chemistry of cervical mucous. Stated to last five years, but requires total cost at application, with charge to remove rods. Often causes irregular bleeding, light to heavy. Removal can possibly cause some scarring.

Rhythm method. Abstinence from intercourse during the woman's fertile days as determined by her menstrual cycle.

Vaginal foam, jelly, suppositories, etc. Nonprescription products for the female that are applied within the vagina. Most contain spermicide—a chemical substance that destroys sperm cells.

Note: Like the morning-after pill, abortifacient RU-486 does not prevent conception. However, it long has been used in Europe as a birth-control method. When taken shortly after the first missed menstrual period, RU-486 causes the newly attached embryo to detach from the lining of the uterus and subsequently to slough off with the menstrual flow.

Copulation (kop-you-LAY-shun) See Coitus.

Cowper's Glands (KAW-perz) Two small glands, one on each side of the male urethra, that secrete a part of the seminal fluid.

Cunnilingus (kun-i-LING-us) The act of applying mouth or tongue to the vulva and clitorts, to sexually stimulate the female.

D & C (Dilation and Curettage) A medical procedure in which the cervix is dilated and a spoon-shaped medical instrument called a curette is used to scrape the lining of the uterus.

Delivery The process of giving birth.

Depo-Provera See Contraception.

Diaphragm See Contraception.

Douche (doosh) The cleaning of the vagina with a stream of liquid solution.

Dysfunction, Sexual See Sexual Dysfunction.

Dysmenorrhea (dis-men-o-REE-ah) Painful menstruation.

Ectopic Pregnancy (ek-TOP-ik) An abnormal pregnancy in which the fetus develops outside the uterus.

Ejaculation (ee-jack-yoo-LAY-shun) The discharge of semen from the penis.

Embryo (EM-bree-oh) The unborn child in its earliest stages of development. In humans, the fertilized ovum during the first eight weeks of its growth.

Endometriosis (en-doh-mee-tree-OH-sis) Condition in which bits of the uterine lining (endometrium) become implanted outside the uterus—in the abdominal cavity, on ovaries, and/or on fallopian tubes. A major cause of infertility. Cause unknown.

Endometrium (en-doe-MEE-tree-um) The lining of the uterus, which monthly thickens and fills with blood in preparation for a fertilized ovum.

Epididymis (ep-ah-DID-i-miss) The mass of tiny coils connecting the testicles with the sperm duct. Sperm are stored here.

Episiotomy (i-pi-zee-AH-toh-mee) An incision made in the vaginal entrance during delivery to facilitate the birth of a child.

Erection (ee-RECK-shun) The enlargement and hardening of the penis or clitoris as tissues fill with blood, usually during sexual excitement.

Erogenous Zone (i-RAH-jenus) Any area of the body that is sexually sensitive or stimulating such as mouth, lips, breast, nipples, and genitals.

Erotic (ee-RAH-tik) Sexually stimulating.

Estrogen (ESS-tro-jen) A hormone that affects functioning of the menstrual cycle and produces female secondary sex characteristics (breast development, widened hips, etc.).

Eunuch (YOO-nuck) A castrated male.

Exhibitionist (ex-i-BISH-un-ist) A person who compulsively exposes his or her sex organs in public.

Extramarital (ex-tra-MARE-i-tal) "Outside of marriage"; often used to refer to illicit sexual intercourse: e.g., "extramarital affair."

Fallopian Tube (fa-LOW-pee-an) The tube through which the egg passes from each ovary to the uterus.

Fellatio (fel-LAY-show) The act of applying the mouth or tongue to the penis to stimulate the male.

Fertility (fer-TILL-i-tee) The ability to reproduce.

Fertilization (fer-till-i-ZAY-shun) Penetration of the ovum by a single sperm, resulting in conception.

Fetus (FEE-tuss) The unborn child from the third month after conception until birth.

Follicle, Ovarian (FAH-li-kull, o-VAIR-ee-an) The small sac near the surface of the ovary that holds the developing egg cell (ovum).

Foreplay The beginning stage of sexual intercourse, during which partners may kiss, caress, and touch each other in order to achieve full sexual arousal.

Foreskin The loose skin covering the tip of the penis, removed during circumcision. Also called the prepuce (PREE-pus).

Fornication (for-ni-KAY-shun) Sexual intercourse between unmarried men and women.

Frigidity (fri-JID-i-tee) Commonly used term for the sexual dysfunction in which a woman is unable to respond to sexual stimulation.

Gene (jean) The carrier for hereditary traits in chromosomes.

Genital Herpes (JEN-i-tal HERP-ease) Sexually transmitted viral disease. Causes open sores on genitalia. Although some medicines may relieve symptoms, there is no cure.

Genital Warts Sexually transmitted viral disease. Causes warts on genitalia. May lead to cancer of the reproductive organs.

Genitalia (jen-i-TAIL-ya) (Genitals; Genital Organs) Visible reproductive or sex organs. Usually denotes vagina, vulva, and clitoris in females and the penis and testicles in males.

Gestation (jes-TAY-shun) The period from conception to birth; in humans, approximately nine months.

Glans (glanz) The head of the penis, exposed when the foreskin is pushed back, or after circumcision.

Gonads (GO-nads) Sex glands—testicle (male), ovaries (female).

Gonorrhea (gon-er-EE-uh) Sexually transmitted bacterial disease. May lead to impotence and/or infertility.

Gynecologist (guy-na-KOLL-o-jist) A physician who specializes in the treatment of female sexual and reproductive organs.

Heredity Traits Characteristics or diseases transmitted from parents to children.

Hermaphrodite (her-MAF-ro-dite) An individual born with both male and female sex organs.

HIV (Human Immunodeficiency Virus) The virus that causes AIDS. Testing HIV positive means the individual's blood contains antibodies indicating HIV infection, but not full-blown AIDS. HIV negative means that at the time of testing no antibodies are present.

Homosexual (ho-mo-SECK-shoo-al) One who is sexually attracted to or sexually active with persons of one's own sex.

Hormone (HOR-moan) A chemical substance, produced by an endocrine gland, that has a particular effect on the function of other organs in the body.

Human Immunodeficiency Virus (HIV) The virus that causes AIDS.

Human Papilloma Virus (HPV) The virus that causes genital warts.

Hymen (HIGH-men) A thin membrane that partially closes the entrance to the vagina. Sometimes called the maidenhead.

Hysterectomy (hiss-ter-ECK-toh-mee) Surgical removal of the uterus.

Hysterotomy (hiss-ter-OT-o-mee) See Abortion.

Impotence (IM-po-tens) A type of male sexual dysfunction; inability to achieve or maintain erection of the penis during sexual intercourse.

Incest (IN-sest) Sexual intercourse between close relatives such as father and daughter, mother and son, or brother and sister.

Infertility (in-fer-TILL-i-tee) Diagnosis arrived at when both husband and wife are healthy and wife does not conceive after one year of intercourse unprotected by contraceptives. (For females who've been on the birth control pill, an extra three months is added to that baseline period.)

Intercourse, Sexual See Coitus.

Intrauterine Device (IUD) (in-trah-YOU-ter-in) A small metal or plastic device inserted into the uterus by a physician and left in place. Abortive in character in that it is thought to prevent a fertilized ovum from being implanted in the uterus and continuing its development. IUD users are at some risk to develop pelvic inflammatory disease, which can result in later tubal pregnancy or even sterility.

In Vitro Fertilization (in VEE-trow fer-till-i-ZAY-shun) Process whereby an egg is removed from the female's ovary, fertilized with the male's sperm in the laboratory, and then implanted into the female's uterus. (Either egg or sperm may have been frozen for storage.)

IUD See Intrauterine Device

Jock Itch A fungus infection causing irritation in the genital area.

Labor (LAY-burr) The stage of giving birth in which the woman's cervix gradually dilates, thus allowing strong contractions of the uterine muscles to push the baby through the vagina and out of the mother's body.

Lactation (lak-TAY-shun) The production and secretion of milk by the mammary glands in the mother's breasts, following childbirth. The process continues as long as the mother nurses her child.

Laparoscopy (lah-pah-ROS-ko-pee) See sterilization.

Lesbian (LEZ-be-an) A female homosexual.

Libido (li-BEE-doe) See Sex Drive.

Maidenhead See Hymen.

Masochism (MASS-o-kizm) Cruelty to self; receiving sexual pleasure from having pain inflicted or by being harshly dominated.

Masturbation (mass-ter-BAY-shun) Self-stimulation of one's sex organs, to the point of orgasm.

Menarche (me-NAR-kee) The onset of the menstrual cycle.

Menopause (MEN-o-pawz) (Change of Life; Climacteric) The end of menstruation in women, usually between the ages of 45 and 55.

Menstruation (men-stroo-AY-shun) The discharge through the vagina of blood from the uterus. This menstrual "period" occurs every 28 to 30 days in females, between puberty and menopause.

Midlife Crisis Term for the change of life (climacteric) in men; sometimes called male menopause. May evoke feelings of restlessness and failure.

Midwife Person capable of caring for woman's gynecological needs and aiding in delivery of infants. Usually a female nurse with additional medical training, who has been certified and has passed the individual state's requirements. (This may not be true of all.) Many work with obstetricians. Legal status varies from state to state.

Miscarriage (MISS-kare-ij) (Spontaneous Abortion) The natural expulsion of a fetus from the uterus, before it is mature enough to live outside the womb, usually due to some abnormal development.

Monilia (mon-ILL-yah) (Yeast Infection) A yeast-like fungus that invades the vagina, causing itching and inflammation. Often spread through sexual contact, but also results from vaginal douching or use of antibiotics.

Morning-after Pill See Abortion.

Narcissism (NAR-su-si-zum) Excessive love of self; egotism; sexual desire or admiration for one's own body.

Nocturnal Emission (nok-TER-nal ee-MISH-un) (Wet Dream) Involuntary male erection and ejaculation during sleep.

Norplant See Contraception.

Nymphomaniac (nim-foe-MAY-nee-ack) A female who experiences excessive sexual desire.

Obstetrician (ob-ste-TRISH-un) A physician who specializes in the care of women during pregnancy, childbirth, and immediately after.

Oral Sex See Cunnilingus; Fellatio.

Orgasm (OR-gazm) (Climax) The peak of excitement in sexual activity.

Ovaries (OH-va-rees) The two female sex glands found on either side of the uterus, in which the ova (egg cells) are formed. They also produce hormones that influence female body characteristics.

Ovulation (ah-vyoo-LAY-shun) Release of the mature (ripe) ovum from the ovary to the fallopian tube.

Ovum (OH-vum) (Plural: ova) Female reproductive cell (egg) found in the ovary. After fertilization by a sperm, the human egg develops into an embryo and then a fetus.

Pedophile (PED-oh-file) A person (usually male) who is sexually aroused by children.

Penis (PEE-nis) Male sex organ through which semen is discharged and urine is passed.

PID (Pelvic Inflammatory Disease) Infection involving female reproductive organs. Often leaves permanent damage resulting in later tubal pregnancies, infertility, and/or sterility. Often linked with untreated STD or use of an IUD.

Pill, The See Contraception.

Pituitary (pih-TOO-it-air-ee) A gland at the base of the brain that controls functions of all the other ductless glands, especially sex glands, adrenals, and thyroid.

Placenta (pluh-SEN-ta) The sponge-like organ that connects the fetus to the lining of the uterus by means of the umbilical cord. It serves to feed the fetus and to dispose of waste. Expelled from the uterus after the birth of a child (afterbirth).

PMS (Premenstrual Syndrome) Discomfort felt by some females for 7 to 14 days prior to menstrual period. Caused by fluctuations in hormone levels.

Pornography (por-NOG-raf-ee) Literature, motion pictures, art, or other means of expression, that, without any concern for personal or moral values, intend simply to be sexually arousing.

Postpartum (post-PAR-tum) Following childbirth.

Pregnancy (PREG-nan-see) Period from conception to birth; the condition of having a developing embryo or fetus within the female body.

Premature Ejaculation (ee-jack-yoo-LAY-shun) A form of sexual dysfunction in which the man ejaculates before, while, or just after inserting the penis into the vagina.

Prenatal (pree-NAY-tal) Before birth.

Prepuce (PREE-pus) See Foreskin.

Progesterone (pro-JES-te-roan) (Progestin) The female "pregnancy hormone" that prepares the uterus to receive the fertilized ovum.

Promiscuous (pro-MISS-kyoo-us) Engaging in sexual intercourse with many persons; engaging in casual sexual relationships.

Prophylactic (pro-fill-ACK-tic) A device or drug used to prevent disease, often specifically sexually transmitted disease. Common term for the condom.

Prostate (PRAH-state) Male gland that surrounds the urethra and neck of the bladder and secretes part of the seminal fluid.

Prostitute (PRAH-sti-toot) An individual who engages in sexual activity for money.

Puberty (PYOO-ber-tee) The period of rapid development that marks the end of childhood; sex organs mature and produce either ova or sperm; the girl becomes a young woman and the boy a young man.

Pubic (PYOO-bik) Regarding the lower part of the abdominal area, specifically where hair grows in a triangular patch.

Rape (rayp) Forcible sexual intercourse with a person who does not consent.

Rectum (RECK-tum) The lower end of the large intestine, ending at the anus.

Rhythm Method See Contraception.

RU-486 See Contraception.

Sadism (SADE-izm) Cruelty; receiving sexual pleasure by inflicting pain on the sexual partner.

Safe Period The interval in the menstrual cycle when the female is presumably not ovulating and therefore is less likely to become pregnant.

Scrotum (SKRO-tum) The sac of skin suspended between the male's legs that contains the testicles.

Semen (SEE-men) (Seminal Fluid, Seminal Emission) The fluid made up of sperm and secretions from the seminal vesicles, prostate, Cowper's glands, and the epididymis. Ejaculated through the penis when the male reaches orgasm.

Seminal Vesicles (SEM-i-nal VESS-i-kals) Provide a nutrient for sperm (which is produced in the testicles). Located on either side of the prostate, they are attached to and open into the sperm ducts.

Sex Drive (Libido) The desire for sexual activity.

Sex, Oral See Cunnilingus; Fellatio.

Sex Organs Commonly refers to the male's penis and female's vagina.

Sexual Dysfunction (SEK-shoo-al dis-FUNK-shun) General term covering problems in sexual performance.

Sexual Intercourse (SEK-shoo-al IN-ter-kors) See Coitus.

Sexually Transmitted Disease (STD) Any of a variety of contagious diseases contracted almost entirely by sexual intercourse. Some of the most common are AIDS, chancroid, chlamydia, genital herpes, genital warts, HIV, gonorrhea, trichomoniasis, and syphilis.

Smegma (SMEG-mah) A thick accumulation of secretions under the foreskin of the penis or around the clitoris; has an unpleasant odor.

Sodomy (SAH-dah-mee) Any of a variety of sexual behaviors, broadly defined by law as deviant, such as sexual intercourse by humans with animals, mouth-genital contact, or anal intercourse between human beings.

Sperm The male reproductive cell(s), produced in the testicles, having the capacity to fertilize the female ova, resulting in pregnancy.

Sperm Bank A storage facility for donor sperm that is used in artificial insemination.

Spermatic Duct (sper-MAT-ik) (Vas Deferens) The tube in the male through which sperm passes from the epididymis to the seminal vesicles and urethra.

Spermatic Cord The tube in the male by which the testicle is suspended; contains the sperm ducts, veins, and nerves.

Spermicide (SPER-mah-side) See Contraception.

Sponge, The See Contraception.

Spontaneous Abortion See Miscarriage.

STD (Sexually Transmitted Disease) More precise term for venereal disease.

Sterility (ster-ILL-it-ee) The inability to reproduce.

Sterilization (ster-ill-ih-ZAY-shun) A procedure by which a male or female is rendered unable to produce children, but can still engage in sexual intercourse. The following are some of the most common surgical methods:

Laparoscopy (la-pa-ROS-ko-pee). Tiny incisions in the abdomen, through which the fallopian tubes are cut or cauterized. Also called "Band-Aid Sterilization."

Tubal ligation/Occlusion. Procedures that cut or seal the fallopian tubes to prevent passage of eggs from ovaries into area where fertilization usually occurs. Technique may be via laparoscopy, posterior colpotomy (approach through the rear of the vagina), or through a minilaparotomy (incision just above the line of pubic hair). Sometimes reversible.

Vasectomy. The male sperm-carrying duct is cut, part is removed, and the ends tied.

Surrogate Mother (SUR-ah-gate) A woman who agrees to become pregnant through artificial insemination (often for a fee) and to carry the fetus to term for an infertile couple. The sperm is usually that of the husband.

Syphilis (SIF-uh-lus) Sexually transmitted bacterial disease. If untreated, can cause systemic damage throughout the body.

Testes (TES-teez) (Testicles) The two male sex glands that produce sperm, suspended within a sac of skin (scrotum) between the legs.

Testosterone (tes-TOSS-ter-own) Male sex hormone produced by the testes; causes and maintains male secondary sex characteristics (voice change, hair growth, etc.).

Toxic Shock Syndrome (TSS) (TOCK-sik shok SIN-drome) Bacterial disease that affects women and men. Flu-like symptoms may be mild or severe, often with rash resembling sunburn. Sometimes associated with high absorbency tampons; failure to change tampons frequently; diaphragm left in place longer than eight hours, or contraceptive sponges.

Transgenderist (trans-JEN-der-ist) A person who identifies very strongly with the other sex and may dress in the clothing of that sex.

Transsexual (trans-SECK-shoo-al) One who feels psychologically like a member of the other sex and is willing to undergo "sex change" surgery to achieve the outward appearance of the other sex.

Transvestite (trans-VES-tite) One who has a compulsion to dress in the clothing of the other sex.

Trichomoniasis (trick-uh-muh-NY-uh-sis) Sexually transmitted one-celled organism that causes vaginal infections.

Trimester (TRY-mess-ter) A period of three months. The nine months of pregnancy are usually divided into trimesters.

Tubal Ligation/Occlusion (too-bul lie-GAY-shun/oh-KLEW-zhun) See Sterilization.

Twins Two children who develop together in the same womb. There are two types of twins:
Fraternal twins. Two children, developed from two separate ova, fertilized by two separate sperm, usually at the same time.
Identical twins. Two children, developed from single ovum, fertilized by a single sperm.

Umbilical Cord (um-BILL-ih-kal) The cord connecting the fetus to the placenta in the womb, through which the fetus receives nourishment.

Urethra (yoo-REE-thra) The duct through which urine passes from the bladder and is eliminated from the body.

Urine (YER-in) A body's liquid waste, manufactured by the kidneys from water and waste materials in the blood, stored in the bladder, and eliminated through the urethra.

Urologist (yoo-RAHL-i-jist) A physician who specializes in treating urinary tract problems of both sexes, as well as the genital tract of males.

Uterus (YOO-ter-us) (Womb) The small, muscular, pear-shaped female organ in which the fetus develops; has the ability to accommodate the growing child (children).

Vagina (vuh-JY-na) (Birth Canal) The canal in the female body between the uterus and the vulva; receives the penis during intercourse; the infant passes through it at birth.

Vasectomy (vuh-SEK-toh-mee) See Sterilization.

Venereal Disease (VD) (veh-NEAR-ee-al) See Sexually Transmitted Disease.

Virgin (VER-jin) A person who has never had sexual intercourse.

Vulva (VUL-va) The female's external sex organs, including the labia majora and labia minora, the outer and inner folds of skin (lips) surrounding the vagina and clitoris.

Wasserman Test (WAHS-er-man) A blood test to determine present or past infection with syphilis.

Wet Dream See Nocturnal Emission.

Womb (WOOM) See Uterus.

X Chromosome A chromosome that determines sex, present in all female ova and in one-half of a male's sperm. If the egg is fertilized by a sperm having an X chromosome, a female will be conceived (XX).

Y Chromosome A sex-determining chromosome present in one-half of a male's sperm. If an ovum is fertilized by a sperm with a Y chromosome, a male will be conceived (XY).

Zygote (ZY-goat) The single cell that results from the union of the sperm and egg at conception. Another term for the fertilized egg.

Index